SOUNDS
IN THE AIR

SOUNDS
IN THE AIR

THE GOLDEN AGE
OF RADIO

Norman H. Finkelstein

CHARLES SCRIBNER'S SONS • NEW YORK
Maxwell Macmillan Canada • Toronto
Maxwell Macmillan International
New York • Oxford • Singapore • Sydney

Charles Scribner's Sons Books for Young Readers
Macmillan Publishing Company • 866 Third Avenue, New York, NY 10022

Maxwell Macmillan Canada, Inc.
1200 Eglinton Avenue East, Suite 200, Don Mills, Ontario M3C 3N1

Macmillan Publishing Company is part of the
Maxwell Communication Group of Companies.

First edition   10   9   8   7   6   5   4   3   2   1
Printed in the United States of America
Book design by Kathryn Parise

Library of Congress Cataloging-in-Publication Data
Finkelstein, Norman H.
Sounds in the air : the golden age of radio / Norman H. Finkelstein. — 1st ed.
        p.   cm.   Includes bibliographical references (p.   ).
Summary: A history of radio's effects on American society in the 1930s and 1940s.
ISBN 0-684-19271-3
1. Radio broadcasting—United States—History—Juvenile literature.
[1. Radio broadcasting—History.]   I. Title.
PN1991.3.U6F56   1993   384.54′09—dc20   92-25354

*For my parents, Sydney and Mollie,
who introduced me to Atwater Kent,
Gabriel Heatter, and The Shadow.*

Acknowledgments

I am grateful to the following for their assistance during my research visits: Ms. Ruth Leonard, Librarian, Mr. Henry Mattoon, Archivist, and Mr. Martin Getzler, Assistant, the American Library of Radio and Television at the Thousand Oaks Library, California; Ms. Cathy Lim, NBC Information Services, New York; Ms. Laura Kapnick, Director, CBS Reference Library, New York; the staffs of the Department of Special Collections, University Research Library, University of California at Los Angeles; the Museum of Television and Radio, New York; Butler Library, Columbia University, New York; Mugar Library, Boston University, Boston. Thanks also to Ms. Elizabeth Adkins, Archives Manager, Kraft General Foods, Inc., and Mr. Michael Projansky.

Grateful acknowledgment is made to the following for permission to quote from copyrighted material:

Bart Andrews for quotations from *Holy Mackeral!: The Amos 'n' Andy Story* by Bart Andrews and Ahrgus Juilliard. Copyright © 1986 by Bart Andrews and Ahrgus Juilliard.

Acknowledgments

CBS, Inc., for quotations from selected CBS News broadcasts. Copyright © 1943, 1965 by CBS, Inc.

John Dunning for quotations from *Tune in Yesterday* by John Dunning. Copyright © 1976 by John Dunning.

Oxford University Press for quotations from *Radio Comedy* by Arthur Frank Wertheim. Copyright © 1979 by Oxford University Press.

Smithsonian Institution Press for quotations from *On the Air* by Amy Henderson. Copyright © 1988 by Smithsonian Institution.

Warner Books, Inc., for quotations from *Sunday Nights at Seven* by Joan Benny. Copyright © 1990 by Joan Benny.

Contents

Contents

x

SOUNDS
IN THE AIR

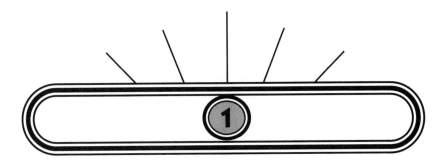

The "Radio Music Box"

The idea is to bring music into the house by wireless.

DAVID SARNOFF

At first he could hardly make out the message. Static and competing sounds made it difficult for the young telegraph operator to hear the faint dots and dashes coming through the headset. From the moment David Sarnoff deciphered the words, he and the rest of the world would never be the same. It was the night of April 14, 1912, and the heart-stopping message was from a ship fourteen hundred miles away at sea. "SS *Titanic* ran into iceberg. Sinking fast." For the next three days and nights Sarnoff stayed at his post, passing information about the disaster to an eager public.

Sarnoff's information came through the wireless telegraph, a new invention most people thought had limited use. It was an outgrowth of pioneer communication technologies invented during the nineteenth century. By mid-century Samuel F. B. Morse had perfected the telegraph, a system for relaying messages over long distances. The system used a series of electrically transmitted dots and dashes to form words. In 1876 the world was stunned when Alexander Graham Bell demonstrated that the human voice could be transmitted from one location to another through use of the telephone. Although sound could now travel over long distances in the United States—and to Europe by an underwater cable—the telegraph and the telephone shared a similar limitation. Both depended on a wire to connect sender and receiver.

A number of inventors and tinkerers worked on ways to transmit sounds through the air, building on the work of two noted European physicists, James Clerk Maxwell and Heinrich Hertz. In 1873 Maxwell, a Scottish scientist, published his theory of electromagnetic waves. It was not until 1886 that Hertz proved Maxwell's theory correct by generating radio waves electrically. From that point the race was on to find a way to utilize that knowledge to transmit sound long distances through the air without using wires or cables.

Although others tried, credit for that feat belongs to the Italian inventor Guglielmo Marconi. In 1896 he was issued a patent in England for his invention, the wireless telegraph. Within a few years his system was in widespread use and the Marconi Wireless Telegraph and Signal Company was a thriving business. By 1899 Marconi was routinely transmitting messages across the English Channel. Two years later, he demonstrated the power of wireless to connect distant places. While he waited patiently at a wireless station in Newfoundland, Canada, the Morse code symbol for the letter S—three dots—was clearly transmitted over the Atlantic Ocean from a wireless station in England. The world suddenly became a smaller place.

Shipowners and the world's navies were the first to recognize the importance of this discovery. No longer were ships at sea isolated. Now, whenever trouble arose, they could call for immediate help. To service the needs of the United States Navy, the American Marconi Company was established.

At the beginning of the twentieth century most people could not imagine that the human voice would ever replace Morse code. But a few engineers and hobbyists continued to experiment with the new wireless technology. While none could successfully compete with the dominance of Marconi, small independent wireless companies were organized. Soon, thanks to pioneer work by Ernst Alexanderson of the General Electric Company, large alternators were built, which allowed sounds to be transmitted over longer distances.

On Christmas Eve 1906 wireless operators on land and sea tapped their headphones in disbelief. Over the usual dots and dashes, they thought they heard music and the sound of a human voice. It was no dream. From a small wireless station in Brant Rock, Massachusetts, Professor Reginald Fessenden was making the first known "broadcast." Fessenden's "show" was little more than phonograph music and the sound of a man singing into a crude microphone. Those few people who heard it could not believe their ears.

It is Lee De Forest, however, who receives credit for the invention that made large-scale broadcasting possible. In 1906 he developed the vacuum tube, which amplified sound. In 1910, to demonstrate the potential of his invention, De Forest put microphones on the stage of New York's Metropolitan Opera House and broadcast the singing voices of the century's two greatest opera stars, Enrico Caruso and Emmy Destinn. The wireless operator on board the SS *Avon* at sea was dumbfounded. An unearthly sound of human singing was clearly coming out of his headset! For the next decade hobbyists continued playing with their electrical toys, perfecting the transmission of sound over the air.

By 1917 there were over eight thousand licensed broadcasters in the United States. Most did not see any applications of wireless technology beyond broadcasting between ship and shore and communicating experimentally among themselves.

David Sarnoff went to work for the American Marconi Company in 1906. He was fifteen years old and wanted to be a telegraph operator.

David Sarnoff *(left)* and Guglielmo Marconi *(right)* visit the RCA Communication Transmitting Center on Long Island, New York, in 1933. *National Portrait Gallery, Smithsonian Institution.*

Because of his age and lack of experience, his first assignment was as an office boy. He bought a telegraph key and spent every spare minute perfecting his Morse code transmitting skills. Soon after he began working at the company, young Sarnoff met the legendary Marconi and impressed the inventor with his zeal and self-taught knowledge. Sarnoff's future in the company was assured.

The crucial role played by wireless telegraphy in the *Titanic* disaster resulted in growth for the Marconi Company and for David Sarnoff, who envisioned a role for the wireless beyond the transmission of business messages over long distances. He was the first to see the potential of radio as a public entertainment and information source.

Four years after the *Titanic* disaster, Sarnoff, promoted to an inspector's position, sent a memo to his superiors about his idea for a "Radio Music Box": "I have in mind a plan of development that would make radio a household utility in the same sense as the piano or phonograph. The idea is to bring music into the home by wireless . . . also events of natural importance can be simultaneously announced and received." None of his bosses shared Sarnoff's dream; the memo was ignored.

Interest in "wireless telephony" by experimenters and engineers continued to grow right up until the entry of the United States into World War I in 1917. Yet only a few lone visionaries like Sarnoff foresaw a role for radio beyond the "message" business. During the war, the United States government, recognizing the strategic importance of wireless broadcasting, took control of all stations in the country. When the war ended, the government saw the need for a unified wireless industry, but there were so many competing companies controlling differing patents that standardization seemed impossible.

In 1919, under pressure from the Navy Department, the General Electric Company sponsored the creation of the Radio Corporation of America (RCA). This powerful company unified the technologies of General Electric, American Telephone and Telegraph, Westinghouse, and the United Fruit Company to provide overseas wireless communication by an American-owned company. Unable to compete because of its British ownership, American Marconi merged into the new larger company. David Sarnoff, now an employee of RCA, dusted off his "Radio Music Box" memo and submitted it to his new bosses at RCA. They liked the young man's idea about radio as a public entertainment source: It gave them a way to sell more radios. In fact, by the end of 1922, RCA's income was more than three times greater from selling radio sets than from the wireless communication service it had been organized to provide.

Small unregulated stations began to spring up all over the country. Some were affiliated with university engineering departments, others with large electronics companies. Radio enthusiasts built their own radio sets, while those less technically inclined bought mass-produced sets. In Pittsburgh, Dr. Frank Conrad of the Westinghouse Electric Company began broadcasting from the garage of his house as a hobby. His little programs of music and baseball scores attracted such a large local following that a Pittsburgh department store soon ran newspaper advertisements offering radios for sale so that customers could listen to Dr. Conrad's programs.

Seeing the business potential, Westinghouse built its own broadcasting station at its factory to promote the sale of its radio receivers. On November 2, 1920, station KDKA began its first broadcast with the announcement of presidential election returns. After the election, KDKA set aside one hour each night for a regularly scheduled broadcast. Soon that hour was expanded, and Westinghouse opened stations near its other factories.

At the end of that year there were thirty licensed broadcasting stations in the United States. Within three years the number of stations grew to over six hundred, and an increasing number of American homes had radio sets. Those early sets did not have speakers. Listeners used headphones to hear sounds from their radios. Until the mid-1920s

6

America was still a "quiet" country. Sounds from blaring radios and televisions that we take for granted today in our homes, automobiles, and streets were unknown and unheard. Most of the early stations were nothing more than low-powered amateur undertakings broadcasting from homes, garages, and factories. Their broadcasts were haphazard and erratic and depended heavily on music to fill the time. Microphones were placed near phonograph loudspeakers, and records were played over the air. Interestingly, large numbers of musicians gladly appeared live on many stations. They worked without pay for either the free publicity or the thrill of participating in the new national craze.

Rudimentary "chains" were formed using telephone lines to share broadcasts among stations. In 1921 station WJZ in Newark broadcast the baseball World Series between the Giants and the Yankees and shared that broadcast with WGY in Schenectady, New York. In 1923 a football game was broadcast jointly by WEAF in New York and WNAC in Boston. In June of that year a speech by President Warren Harding was broadcast in several cities at the same time to an audience of one million. Clearly, something had to be done to organize the industry. Again, it was David Sarnoff who came up with a solution.

Sarnoff's newest idea was for RCA to create a national broadcasting company to permanently link together a large number of local stations around the country. In 1921 he proved the potential of attracting large audiences by broadcasting the heavyweight championship fight between Jack Dempsey and Georges Carpentier. An estimated three hundred thousand people tuned in. By making quality programming available to larger numbers of listeners, RCA could sell more radios. They were prohibited by law from selling broadcast time or advertising, so their profits came exclusively from the sale of radio sets. There was, however, a problem with competition.

In 1922 the American Telephone and Telegraph Company (AT&T) opened its own station, WEAF, in New York. It skirted the advertising limitations of the RCA stations by treating public broadcasting as an extension of telephone service. Just as the telephone provided only the *means* to communicate—people could say anything they wished in their phone conversations—AT&T provided only broadcast *time*, not programs. It offered to sell chunks of airtime to advertisers, who in turn were responsible for filling their allotted time.

The first advertisement aired over WEAF on August 28, 1922, when a local real estate company bought ten minutes for fifty dollars to sell apartments. The instant business success led to other advertisers buying time, and the age of the commercial message was born. Soon other stations joined with WEAF to form a small chain. The RCA-affiliated stations, prohibited from selling time directly, devised their own method of handling advertising. They gave airtime free to advertisers with the understanding that the sponsors would pay all costs associated with putting the programs on the air, including payments to performers.

In 1925 Sarnoff negotiated a deal with AT&T in which the telephone company agreed to withdraw from the broadcasting business and turn its stations over to RCA. In return, RCA agreed to lease telephone lines exclusively from AT&T to connect their stations across the country. On September 9, 1926, RCA incorporated the National Broadcasting Company (NBC). Using the blue cables that connected the old RCA stations and the red cables of the previous AT&T stations, it linked the old RCA stations together as the NBC Blue Network and the former AT&T stations as the NBC Red Network. On November 15, 1926, both new networks were inaugurated with a gala simultaneous broadcast from New York's Waldorf-Astoria Hotel, with a listening audience of more than twelve million.

In 1927 another network was formed when William S. Paley joined together sixteen failing radio stations as the Columbia Broadcasting System (CBS). Two years later, CBS had seventy stations and was clearing a yearly profit of over two million dollars. Paley, like Sarnoff, had a vision of what broadcasting could become. Only large networks could have the economic clout to bring the finest entertainment to the listening public.

During that first season of network programming, 1926–1927, the broadcast model that lasted into the 1950s was developed. Most programs carried the names of sponsors and leaned heavily on music and variety entertainment. On Tuesday nights at nine there was the "Eveready Hour" on the NBC Red Network. Thursday nights brought the "Maxwell House Coffee Hour" on NBC Blue. Mondays at nine the A & P Gypsies sang; the Ipana Troubadours performed on Wednesdays.

The major networks developed different ways of dealing with their affiliated stations. NBC charged member stations a fee for each sustaining (unsponsored) program and paid them for each sponsored network program they chose to broadcast. At CBS, both sustaining and sponsored network programs were free to the affiliated stations, with the network responsible for selling airtime to national advertisers. The CBS stations liked this arrangement; they didn't need to worry about programming. William Paley liked it because he could approach prospective national advertisers with a fixed schedule of times and stations.

The rapid growth of radio created unanticipated regulatory problems. Stations broadcast on the same frequencies and agreements to share airtime were regularly broken. Radio sales began to drop as listeners heard only conflicting sounds from competing stations. Congress was forced to intervene with the Radio Act of 1927. It created the Federal Radio Commission (today known as the Federal Communications Commission) to set up and enforce rules and regulations for American broadcasting. The American broadcasting industry had survived a difficult birth and was about to enter its most glorious years.

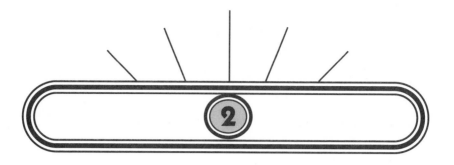

Vaudeville of the Airways

I love to spend one hour with you.

EDDIE CANTOR'S THEME SONG

To those of us accustomed to cable television, video games, satellite dishes, and VCRs, the content and style of early radio broadcasts might seem slightly amateurish. In fact, they were. In 1920 there were no broadcasting standards or examples to follow. The industry invented itself as it went along. Every innovation was a milestone. For the growing number of headphone-wearing listeners, the prime thrill was being able to listen to anything. Program content was secondary as people hunched over hard-to-tune crystal radio sets, trying to separate meaningful sound from static.

People who liked music were in luck. Most of the early broadcasts consisted of live musical selections. As a typical example, WFAA of Dallas, Texas, on the evening of October 22, 1922, presented, in succession, a baritone solo, a piano concerto, a vocal solo, and a selection from the opera *La Boheme*.

Sports programs played an important role from the beginning. A World Series baseball game was broadcast for the first time on October 21, 1921. It was not a live, at-the-ballpark presentation. Instead, a reporter at the game telephoned the action to a studio announcer miles away, who broadcast the information to the listeners.

Ronald Reagan, later to become president of the United States, began his show-business career as a sports announcer. He often told of his need to dramatize reports with created scenarios to keep his listeners' attention.

Special broadcasts soon proved radio's value beyond entertainment. Presidential addresses and political events captured public attention. In 1924 people who owned radios were able to tune in the Democratic National Convention. Never before had ordinary citizens heard a live, ongoing news event.

One of the earliest newscasters was H. V. Kaltenborn, a reporter for the *Brooklyn Daily Eagle* who first spoke on the air in 1921 over WJZ. His commentary on the news was so successful that the newspaper was asked to contribute further talks by him.

Radio had an insatiable thirst for performers to fill the vast airtime. Music, both live and recorded, occupied much of a listener's attention. By 1926, when nearly three-quarters of all radio owners tuned in at least once a day, up to 90 percent of broadcasting time consisted of music in one form or another. The sale of records dropped by more than 80 percent; radio was free. A few talk shows began to appear to break up the nearly constant sound of music. One of the earliest such shows was "Roxy and His Gang," led by S. L. ("Roxy") Rothafel, owner of New York's important Capitol Theater. His guests included popular show-business and political figures.

In August 1922, WGY in Schenectady, New York, began broadcasting live plays. While musical talent in the area was limited, actors abounded. Live plays had previously been aired directly from theaters

Radio comedian Eddie Cantor autographs a typical 1930s radio. *Library of Congress.*

as onetime programs, but the regularly broadcast "WGY Players" became a tremendous hit. Between scenes, an orchestra played musical interludes. For the first time, sound effects were used to make radio plays seem even more realistic. Within a year the program was sent live to stations in New York and Washington over Western Union telegraph lines. Now not only the record business but live theater felt the competition of radio.

Radio links over long distances became a common way to cut costs and share talent. At first stations were linked to share specific, or onetime, broadcasts. As the 1920s progressed, these informal station chains developed into the large national radio networks. The creation of the National Broadcasting Company's Red and Blue networks and the founding of CBS resulted in more disciplined use of the airwaves. Gone were spontaneous discussions and amateurish programming. Instead, radio programs were carefully planned, scripted, and auditioned.

Before 1922 fewer than sixty thousand American families owned radios: By 1930 the number had mushroomed to well over thirteen million. The radio itself became more sophisticated. Hard-to-tune crystal sets were replaced by tube sets, which allowed clearer and more precise reception. Also gone were the headphones. Loudspeakers built into the sets allowed an entire family to listen simultaneously to the same program. Indeed, the radio became more than a curiosity in most homes; it was treated as a beautiful piece of furniture and usually occupied a prominent place in the living room.

By 1930 the regionalism that had been so much a part of the American heritage was virtually eliminated. The prophecy of David Sarnoff was coming true. Radio was "creating a new common fund of experience and information that was democratic in its touch-of-the-dial accessibility."

Increasingly the United States became an urban society, if not in the actual size of communities then in taste and outlook. Over time, the networks permitted people all over the country to share the same entertainment, culture, and news. Like no other invention, radio provided Americans with a common cultural experience that ignored social position, race, religion, and educational background.

Unlike the development of radio in other countries, stations in the United States were not funded by either the government or by user taxes, but by advertising. Connecting a large number of widely scattered stations made radio appealing to advertisers, who could now reach larger audiences. Likewise, the spectacular growth of national companies during the 1920s made radio a natural advertising medium. With the infusion of money, talent could be paid and programming could become more diverse.

The way in which the United States traditionally conducted business changed as competition increased. Small, family-owned neighborhood stores gave way to large, nationally affiliated chains. The number of Woolworth stores mushroomed from 1,000 in 1920 to 1,825 by 1929. During that same period, the number of A & P food stores increased from 4,500 to over 15,000. Products and services needed new ways of attracting customers.

The first commercial message, in August 1922, was a ten-minute talk urging listeners in the New York area to rent apartments in a new building complex in Queens named after Nathaniel Hawthorne. The program, not coincidentally, happened to be about Hawthorne, the long-dead but respected American writer. This mixture of advertising with not-too-subtle programming was typical of the time. A program called "The Story of the Christmas Card" was presented by the Greeting Card Association, while a talk by Elwood Haynes, the inventor of the Haynes automobile, was, naturally, sponsored by the Haynes Automobile Company.

In the early years of broadcasting, sponsors backed away from obviously crass commercialization and chose low-key ways of bringing their names to the public. At first they were content just to have their products mentioned in a program's title. Within a few years they took a further step by introducing programs with catchy jingles. Listeners were entertained by "The A & P Gypsies" (food stores), "Clicquot Club Eskimos" (soda pop), "Gold Dust Twins" (laundry detergent), "Ipana Troubadours" (toothpaste), "Silvertown Cord Orchestra" (tires), "The Kodak Chorus" (cameras), the "Atwater Kent Entertainers" (radios), "The Palmolive Hour" (soap), "The Wrigley Hour" (chewing gum), "Stetson Parade" (hats), and "Vicks VapoRub Quartette" (medication).

No radio entertainers underwent as many sponsor changes as two comics, Billy Jones and Ernie Hare. They began on radio in 1921 as "The Happiness Boys," sponsored by the Happiness Candy Company. They went on to be known as the "Interwoven Pair" (socks), the "Flit Soldiers" (insect repellant), the "Best Foods Boys" (mayonnaise), the "Taystee Loafers" (bread), and "Trade and Mark" (Smith Brothers cough drops). No matter who sponsored them, they always began their programs with the same sprightly tune, "How Do You Do, Everybody, How Do You Do?"

The advertising genius of those early days was George Washington Hill, president of the American Tobacco Company. He recognized the unique capability of radio to sell products and proceeded to invent modern broadcast advertising. He was a strong believer in overdosing listeners with snappy jingles repeated loudly and often. In 1928 he decided that radio was the way to convince fashion-conscious women to take up cigarette smoking as a diet aid—not just any cigarette, but American Tobacco's leading brand, Lucky Strike. The slogan he came up with was direct, catchy, and to the point: "Reach for a Lucky instead of a sweet." Sales skyrocketed among women.

Listings of program times and stations began to appear in daily newspapers. Although newspaper owners wished that radio would leave advertising revenues solely to the print media, obviously radio was here to stay. Many newspapers did, however, drop sponsor names from their listings. "The Fleischmann's Hour" became "The Rudy Vallee Show" and the "Lucky Strike Program" was "Rolfe's Orchestra."

Most programs of that era adopted identical bland formulas with a heavy reliance on live music. Radio announcers began as anonymous ad-libbers who filled time between performances, but soon became personalities in their own right. Norman Brokenshire and Milton Cross began as local station announcers and became famous. Other announcers became program hosts. Morning talk shows, directed by cheery and soothing personalities, were among the first programs to break the all-music format. Tony Wons was a favorite with women. He developed a unique and provocative way of intimately whispering into the microphone, "Are you listening?" Women all over the United States felt he was talking to them personally.

To fill even more time, talks and speeches by politicians, ministers, and bureaucrats of all political persuasions were scheduled. The "Ten Outstanding [radio] Events of This Week" as selected by the *New York Times* for June 5 to June 11, 1927, were as follows:

Sunday	9:15	William Simmons, Baritone
Monday	7:30	Roxy and His Gang
	9:00	Gypsies String Ensemble
	10:00	Opera, *Cavalleria Rusticana*
Tuesday	8:30	Goldman Band
	9:00	Eveready Orchestra
Wednesday	9:00	Maxwell Concert Orchestra
	9:30	National Electric Light Conference: Speaker: David F. Houston; Mario Chamlee, Tenor; Olsen's Orchestra

| Friday | 8:30 | Royal Salon Orchestra |
| Saturday | 9:00 | Bureau of the Budget Meeting: Addresses by President Calvin Coolidge and Brigadier General H. M. Lord |

Until the 1930s most stations did not broadcast continuously during the day. Even so, it was difficult to fill the available time. As network affiliations grew, the sloppiness of early broadcasting disappeared. Programs were slotted into exact time frames, measured to the split second. Schedules and scripts were carefully followed.

Broadcast material of all types was needed, although music continued to predominate. Not everyone was pleased with all the musical programs. Speaking at a meeting in New York of the Music Publishers' Association, the organization's president said, "Radio with its superloud speakers and its numerous programs has cheapened music as music . . . it makes music too easy to obtain and consequently too little respected and appreciated. The inevitable result is cheapness of music and the creation of a feeling of disrespect for all that is finest in music."

The gentleman obviously did not understand the power of radio. Indeed, one positive result of all the musical programming was to make the United States more musically aware. In 1927 NBC hired Walter Damrosch, conductor of the New York Symphony Orchestra, to host a "Music Appreciation Hour" over the network. His educational and informative program was received in over one hundred twenty-five thousand classrooms all over the country. Damrosch became one of early radio's most beloved personalities.

The decade following World War I moved America away from its rural heritage. It was a decade of technological growth, when new industries flourished. President Calvin Coolidge, never a man of many words, summed up the progress by saying, "The chief business of America is business." Underlying the unprecedented growth of the American economy were social upheavals just as spectacular. Women got the right to vote. The right to alcoholic beverages was denied, and although Prohibition was doomed to failure, its short existence during the 1920s led to cultural changes. Gangsters like Al Capone and Bugsy Siegal kept the country horrified with headline-making crimes. Jazz music moved from Harlem into mainstream America; everyone danced the Charleston and the black bottom.

Electricity reached into almost every American home. A national highway system covered the length and breadth of the country, providing access to even the remotest village. Indeed, the number of automobiles had grown from fewer than seven million at the turn of the decade to over twenty-three million by 1930. For the daring few, the new airplane phenomenon provided a faster alternative to the railroads.

But it was radio that captured the hearts of America. In an era of national crazes from flagpole sitting to marathon dancing, radio served as the instant dispenser of the latest fads. It was the perfect invention for an exciting time. When Charles A. Lindbergh became the first person to fly across the Atlantic in 1927, it seemed as if the entire country turned to radio for the latest information. His tumultuous ticker tape parade in New York was covered live.

The Roaring Twenties was a period of joyful excess. Aside from the excitement stirred up by Prohibition, the stock market was perhaps the greatest topic of discussion. With each passing year the price of stocks shot higher. Investors borrowed money to buy more shares. Not unexpectedly, RCA stock was among the fastest-rising of the decade. In 1928 a share of RCA stock could be bought for eighty-five dollars. By the summer of 1929 that same share's price had risen to five hundred dollars. The market was the topic of everyday conversation, even among those who were not investing.

Radio stars were so popular that, when they appeared in theaters, they attracted large crowds. This crowd gathered outside a Pittsburgh, Pennsylvania, theater in which radio star Joe Penner was appearing. *American Library of Radio and Television, Thousand Oaks Library.*

As the market rose to dizzying heights, no one imagined the boom ever ending. But end it did, in spectacular fashion. On October 30, 1929, *Variety*, the legendary show-business newspaper, headlined the stock market crash in its own special style: WALL STREET LAYS AN EGG. The country and the world entered the worst economic period in modern history, with high unemployment and a devastated business climate. Banks failed—deposits were not protected by government insurance at that time—and millions of people lost their life's savings. Twenty-five percent of American workers were out of jobs as factories shut down. Breadlines and soup kitchens provided nourishment to the new breed of homeless people.

One of the first entertainment institutions to feel the economic pinch of the Great Depression was vaudeville. For decades it had been the major live theater entertainment for the American public. Vaudeville theaters, organized into chains throughout the country, shared variety acts of every possible type. E. F. Albee, Willie Hammerstein, and B. F. Keith ran their nationwide vaudeville circuits with dictatorial grace. Comedians, singers, jugglers, dog acts, acrobats, and dancers competed with one another for the favor of audiences, thereby earning higher, better-paid positions on the theater bill, or perhaps an opportunity to play the Palace in New York, the most prestigious theater of all.

Vaudeville declined in popularity because of the quickly developing film industry and the economic pressures caused by the Great Depression. Vaudeville houses around the country closed or, like the famous Palace, were transformed into movie theaters. At first, live entertainment and movies shared the same bill. Gradually, films outlived the last of the vaudeville acts.

One of the most successful vaudeville acts at the turn of the century was Gus Edwards's School Days. Edwards, a producer and songwriter who wrote the popular song "School Days" is also credited with having discovered boys and girls who later became leading entertainers. The talented children he hired sang, danced, and exchanged gags to the delight of audiences everywhere. Many of the young performers came directly out of the Lower East Side or other immigrant ghettos of New York.

Vaudeville was a tough business. Those who were not quick on their feet, clever, and tenacious quickly fell by the wayside. The performers who were among the best graduated to acts of their own. Groucho Marx, Eddie Cantor, Walter Winchell, and George Jessel were among the many who got their start in show business this way. When vaudeville died they and others—like Al Jolson, Rudy Vallee, Jack Pearl, George Burns and Gracie Allen, Jack Benny, Ed Wynn, and Fred Allen—transferred their talents to radio. They established the rules and set the standards for what would later be called radio's golden age.

In the fall of 1929 a young singer by the name of Rudy Vallee became the host of a popular weekly hour-long variety show, "The Fleischmann Hour," sponsored by a yeast company. It drew heavily on the talents of former vaudeville stars and downplayed "serious" music. For the entertainers, it was the equivalent of playing the Palace. Listeners loved the informal tone of the program and the light musical entertainment. Vallee himself was an appealing personality. He was a Yale graduate who had played in vaudeville and gone on to lead his own band at New York's Heigh-Ho Club, where he first used his well-known radio greeting, "Heigh-ho, everybody!" He became known as "The Vagabond Lover," after a song he popularized, and developed a unique "crooner" style of singing that strongly affected women.

Other variety shows soon followed. "The Maxwell House Showboat" was the first to have actors play the same radio characters each week. The popular music presented by big bands and famous singers quickly replaced the classical music that had been the staple of radio broadcasting during the 1920s. Listeners enjoyed the music of Guy Lombardo, Kate Smith, Al Jolson, and Bing Crosby.

Rudy Vallee, one of the most popular "crooners" on radio. *American Library of Radio and Television, Thousand Oaks Library, Rudy Vallee Collection.*

Kate Smith was a successful entertainer on Broadway, with a powerful voice. Now, thanks to radio, her beautiful singing was heard all over the country. She began each show with the song that became her radio trademark, "When the Moon Comes over the Mountain." Al Jolson, the son of a cantor, got his start in popular minstrel shows and graduated to vaudeville. Jolson's 1927 film, *The Jazz Singer*, was the first "talking picture." He had a dynamic singing style that no one has ever been able to duplicate. Years later, when a movie was made of his life, he was called out of retirement to sing the songs for the film's sound track.

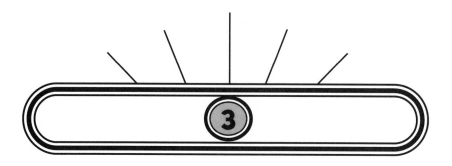

Comedy Tonight

There are three things I'll never forget about America:
the Rocky Mountains, Niagara Falls, and Amos 'n' Andy.

George Bernard Shaw

If music sustained radio during the 1920s, comedy ruled the 1930s. When the Roaring Twenties slid into the Great Depression of the 1930s, something was needed to lift the spirits of the American people. Radio comedy arrived just in time. It all began with "Amos 'n' Andy," the first serial situation comedy. Within months after the first national broadcast, the program was enchanting the entire country. Some movie theaters delayed their evening showings until 7:30; others interrupted their shows and piped the radio program to the audiences. From 7:00 to 7:15 each weekday evening telephone usage dropped by half and sewer superintendents in major cities reported the highest water pressure of the day—no one visited the bathroom! Even President Calvin Coolidge was said to excuse himself from state dinners to listen to the show.

The program's creators, Freeman Gosden and Charles Correll, wrote each episode and performed each of the speaking parts. The program originated on January 12, 1926, when they first broadcast a program called "Sam 'n' Henry" over a local Chicago station. The daily broadcasts dealt with the humorous experiences of African Americans who had migrated north to Chicago from the Deep South. The African-American characters invented by the white Gosden and Correll spoke in heavily stereotyped dialect laced with mispronunciations.

By today's standards "Sam 'n' Henry" would never have been broadcast. Many would consider the show demeaning and insulting to African Americans. During that time of racial insensitivity, however, most African Americans were separated from their white neighbors by ghettos, blatant discrimination, and class differences. Although "Sam 'n' Henry" undoubtedly made some white people feel more intelligent and diligent than their black neighbors, the popularity of the program seems to have been based less on racism than on the universal appeal of characters who were trying to get ahead in America during tough times.

"Sam 'n' Henry" stayed on the air for 586 broadcasts. When Gosden and Correll moved to another Chicago station, WMAQ, in 1928, they had to change the name of the program. The result was "Amos 'n' Andy." They also created a "chainless chain" by developing an innovative transcription network of forty other radio stations. The programs were recorded and sent to the other stations for later broadcast. So popular was the program that Gosden and Correll made live theater appearances in blackface.

In the summer of 1929 "Amos 'n' Andy" went national over the NBC Blue Network, sponsored by Pepsodent toothpaste. Broadcast six days a week, it became the most popular radio show of that era.

Listeners everywhere were caught up in the antics of Amos; Andy;

the Kingfish; the Fresh Air Taxicab Company, "Incorpulated"; and the Mystic Knights of the Sea lodge. The character of Amos—hardworking, decent, honest, and soft-spoken—was always upstaged by the loud, scheming, and conniving George Stevens, the "Kingfish" of the lodge. Once, when the network changed the broadcast time of the program to 11 P.M. to accommodate listeners on the West Coast, the country almost experienced a second revolutionary war. Fans threatened a boycott of Pepsodent toothpaste, and complaint letters by the thousands flooded the network offices. Gosden and Correll volunteered to do two live programs a night, one at seven for the East Coast and one at eleven (8 P.M. on the West Coast) to satisfy the entire country. Some said that if you took a walk down any street in America on a hot summer day when "Amos 'n' Andy" was broadcast, you could listen to the complete program as you passed by each home's open windows.

Like "Amos 'n' Andy," "Rise of the Goldbergs," also sponsored by Pepsodent, presented listeners with a minority group's story. It began as a weekly fifteen-minute sustaining (unsponsored) program on NBC in 1929 before being picked up in 1931 by Pepsodent. Just as "Amos 'n' Andy" made Americans more aware of their African-American neighbors, "The Goldbergs" introduced Jewish people into the most remote towns in the United States, where a Jew had never been seen. Written by Gertrude Berg, who also played Mollie Goldberg, the program's main character, "Rise of the Goldbergs" was the continuing story of Jewish immigrants and their American-born children, Rosalie and Sammy. Heard five times a week, for fifteen minutes a day, it was in many ways the first soap opera.

While the adult characters spoke with accents and Mrs. Goldberg continuously fractured English sentence structure, the emphasis was on a story to which all Americans could relate. "Yoo-hoo, Mrs. Bloom," Mrs. Goldberg shouted to her unseen neighbor, and the night's episode would begin. For the first few years of the program Gertrude Berg played the Mollie character in Yiddish dialect. "Oy, dere's mine bell vot's ringing," or "Vat's de matter so late, Sammy?" Later, the dialect was dropped, but the inverted sentence structure remained.

Other dialect comedians were also popular. Vaudeville had had numerous "Dutchman" acts where the lines were spoken in thick German accents. One of the most popular carryovers was Jack Pearl in his role as Baron Munchausen. As the baron told tall tales, his partner, Charlie, would deflate them. The baron then responded with, "Vas you dere, Sharlie?" and the audience roared. Soon all America was using the expression with delight.

Other groups were represented, too, and ethnic characters abounded on many of the popular shows. "Frank Watanabe and the Honorable Archie" debuted in 1930. Eddie Cantor had The Mad Russian, and Parkyakarkas, a Greek restaurant owner. Al Pearce had Yogi Yorgesson, a Swede; Lily, an African American; and Mr. Kissel, a Jew. Fred Allen had Ajax Cassidy, an Irishman, and Mrs. Nussbaum, a Jew. Jack Benny had Rochester, a part played for years on radio and television by Eddie Anderson, a talented African-American actor. Mr. Schlepperman and Mr. Kitzel, two characters with thick Yiddish accents, often appeared on the show.

By 1933, with the nation deeply in the grip of the depression, vaudeville comics found themselves in great demand for radio. Americans needed to laugh. Radio listenership had dropped dramatically as people tired of the old programming. Even the "Amos 'n' Andy" show had lost its original popularity. The networks looked for new programming to bring back the listeners. They introduced dramatic series like "The Adventures of Sherlock Holmes," "The Shadow," and "Rin-Tin-Tin." These programs increased the number of radio listeners, but what the networks really needed were famous entertainers to attract

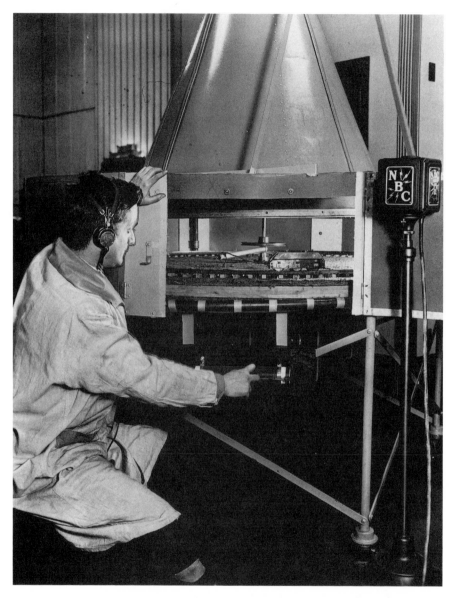

Inside a specially built sound chamber, a toy train provides a realistic sound effect for a radio drama. *Library of Congress.*

even larger audiences. Why pay to develop new talent when unemployed, experienced, and well-known stage stars were now available?

Because of their widespread traveling, successful vaudeville comics had developed a style of humor that played well in all parts of the country. They were experienced men and women who had learned their craft under the most trying conditions. Simply to have survived the demanding audiences was a sign of competence and accomplishment. They loved their lives as comics and it showed when they performed.

The best comics kept their gags and stories simple. They knew from experience that nothing turned an audience off quicker than a complicated story or an insincere delivery. Once on the radio, they learned to present their material without relying on the sight gags that had sustained them on the stage. This meant no more of the funny costumes, suggestive winks, grimaces, or hand motions that had made theater audiences laugh.

Instead radio comedians relied on a second person on the program to act as the "straight man" or "stooge" for jokes, gags, and scenes. The stooge generally took one of three characterizations. First were the wives, often the comedians' real spouses. The most famous husband-and-wife teams were George Burns and Gracie Allen, Fred Allen and Portland Hoffa, and Jack Benny and Mary Livingstone. A second category consisted of foreign-accented stooges like The Mad Russian and Parkyakarkas. Finally, there were the program announcers, many of whom were associated with particular comedians and programs for years: Graham McNamee with Ed Wynn, Harry von Zell with Eddie Cantor, Harlow Wilcox with "Fibber McGee and Molly," and Don Wilson with Jack Benny. These early radio announcers did more than just introduce programs and announce station breaks. They were well-known personalities in their own right, with national recognition and followings.

To today's sophisticated audiences, what passed as humor in the 1930s may seem corny and trite. "I never forgot the time I was fighting a lion single-handed," Jack Pearl's Baron Munchausen told his stooge, Charlie. "Baron, how did you come out?" Charlie asked. "Single handed," the Baron replied. Or how about this one? "I have the smallest radio in the world. My radio is so small that when 'Amos 'n' Andy' is on, all I get is Amos." Comedian Joe Penner's gags were simple. He depended primarily on his delivery and intonation. "What kind of hen lays the longest? A dead one!" Ha-ha-ha. For reasons no psychiatrist has ever explained, one of his lines became classic and evoked sidesplitting laughter whenever it was uttered: "Wanna buy a duck?" Not funny, you say. Yet, in the 1930s that line was perhaps the most famous radio phrase of all.

Ben Bernie, the Old Maestro, had a popular variety show for years. He was a bandleader who supplemented his musical presentations with guests from show business. He had a smooth, sophisticated delivery, although his pronunciation still maintained an obvious trace of Brooklyn. He referred to the audience as "youse guys and youse gals" and made "Yowzuh! Yowzuh!" a national catchword. He always ended his program by reading the same pleasant but corny poem:

Au revoir. Pleasant dreams.
Think of us . . . whenever you request themes . . .
Au revoir, a fond cheerio, a bit of tweet-tweet,
God bless you . . . and pleasant dreams.

Ed Wynn was the Texaco Fire Chief. Wynn, a most successful stage star, had starred in the Ziegfeld Follies and in his own play, *The Perfect Fool*, which in 1922 became the first stage play to be broadcast live on radio. He insisted on doing his radio show in front of a live audience and wore costumes and makeup. As an old vaudevillian, he needed the reaction of people in the studio to make his gags come alive. Trading barbs with his announcer, Graham McNamee, he delivered one gag after another in his unique, high-pitched voice.

Unlike many of the other comedians, who relied on writers for new material, Wynn came to radio with over twenty thousand of his own gags. While a vaudeville comic appearing in different cities could use and reuse material, a radio comic could use a gag just once. Even comedians with a staff of writers had difficulty keeping up with the demands. By the end of the decade, Wynn literally ran out of material, and his popularity sagged. But during most of the time he was on the air, his show was among the most popular.

Another star who needed no introduction to radio audiences was Eddie Cantor. Born on the Lower East Side of New York, Cantor grew up singing and dancing for coins on street corners. After leaving school, he found a job as a singing waiter at Kerry Walsh's saloon in Coney Island. The piano player was Jimmy Durante, later to be a radio

Eddie Cantor was born Edward Isko-witz in 1892 in New York City, the son of poor Russian Jewish immigrants. His talent for mimicry led him into vaudeville and then to Broadway. *National Archives.*

star in his own right. From the saloon, Cantor joined Gus Edwards's Kid Kabaret. In vaudeville he appeared in a number of successful acts, primarily in blackface.

Cantor once recounted a "fan" letter sent to a New York radio station in 1923 after one of his earliest radio appearances: "After hearing Eddie Cantor on your program, whenever you announce that he's going to make another appearance, I'm the first one at the radio— and heaven help anyone who tries to turn it on!"

Early in his career he developed a unique performing style. He later said he did it in order to avoid the fruits and vegetables often thrown at entertainers by less-than-satisfied ticket holders. His trademark act included prancing around the stage at a fast pace, clapping his hands, and goggling his eyes, all the while singing infectious tunes to the delight of the audience. He starred in many films, making songs like "Whoopie!" and "If You Knew Susie" popular hits.

Cantor's radio career, which began in 1931, made him one of broadcasting's most popular stars well into the 1940s. In the mid-1930s he even ousted "Amos 'n' Andy" for the number-one radio program spot. Unlike the story-oriented humor of "Amos 'n' Andy," Cantor used a fast-paced vaudeville style to deliver gags and banter with guest stars he used in place of a permanent cast of performers.

Some of the comedians used their own personal characteristics, either real or created, around which to build humor. Jimmy Durante relied on his large nose. "Here it is, folks! Yes, it's real. It ain't gonna bite ya, but it ain't gonna fall off. Any famous people in da audience can come up and autograph it." Eddie Cantor described Durante's command of the English language in this way: "His grammar and diction would send an English teacher to the nearest bottle marked poison."

Jack Benny developed a reputation as a cheapskate who would walk miles rather than waste an ounce of gasoline or spend a nickel on a bus. In real life he was a generous and charitable person, but his radio reputation could not be shaken.

When NBC and CBS were first formed in the late 1920s, most radio programs were produced by the networks or their affiliated stations. By 1931 nearly all network programs were produced directly by advertising agencies, which were responsible for writing the programs and hiring the staffs. The famous stars, in effect, did not work for the networks, but for the agencies that represented the sponsors. Advertising became the lifeblood of radio, and radio stars were identified with the products of the companies that sponsored them.

Most programs were not prerecorded but went over the air live. Everything had to be timed down to the last second. The famous comedians often ad-libbed during their programs and invariably ran out of time. Jack Benny and Fred Allen usually ended their shows by simply saying, "We're a little late, folks, so good night."

Unlike the theater, radio provided room for clever manipulation of effects. Specialists appeared who used their talents to make programs come alive. If a script called for a dog to bark or a baby to cry, one could not depend upon a dog or a baby in the studio to perform at the split second needed. Talented people who could cry like babies and bark like dogs now had employment. There were even those who excelled in screaming. When the script called for a scream, the specialist stepped up to the microphone and performed, thereby sparing actors from straining their valuable voices.

The most popular programs in the 1930s were the comedy / variety shows. Although sponsorship and broadcast times changed, by 1944 many of the programs had been on the air for more than ten years. If you tuned in to any of these programs, you not only heard the regular commercials, but mention of the sponsor in other ways. Some of the comedians lightly made fun of the sponsor or changed words of popular songs to include the sponsor's product. Jack Benny, when he was spon-

One of the most unbelievable bands ever assembled: Groucho Marx plays guitar; Jack Benny, violin; Eddie Cantor, bass; and George Burns, trombone. *Special Collections Department, University Research Library, UCLA.*

sored by Jell-O, sometimes began his program with "Jell-O, everybody" instead of "hello." It may not have been the dignified approach many sponsors originally wanted for their products, but most did not complain. After all, sales reached new heights.

Fred Allen was one of the most talented comedians. His wry sense of humor developed over a long show-business career. He first went on the air in 1932 on CBS. Allen successfully relied on supporting characters with whom to match wits. His strolls down Allen's Alley, begun in 1941, became classic comedy. As he made his way down the imaginary lane, listeners had the opportunity to meet his varied cast. Mrs. Pansy Nussbaum, played by Minerva Pious, spoke with a heavy Yiddish accent, usually about "mine husband, Pierre." Titus Moody was a crusty New England farmer who always greeted Allen with "Howdy, bub." And there was Senator Beauregard Claghorn, the comic stereotype of an American politician, who spoke with a heavy and exaggerated southern accent: "Somebody, ah say somebody's knockin' on mah door!"

George Burns and his wife, Gracie Allen, were experienced vaudeville stars when they began on radio in 1932. At first, Gracie played straight man to her husband. When George realized that his wife was actually funnier, they reversed roles, and George Burns became the most famous straight man in radio. Gracie, characterized as a pleasant but dim-witted wife, made the most illogical events seem completely understandable.

One of the most famous publicity stunts created on radio was Gracie's search for her "missing" brother. Not only did this "search" keep listeners tuned to the Burns and Allen program, but Gracie also appeared unannounced as a guest on other radio shows. Everyone was looking for the "missing" brother. Meanwhile, not amused by all the sudden attention, Gracie's real brother went into hiding until the gimmick ended.

Singers were also popular radio stars who showcased comedians.

Rudy Vallee and Kate Smith were early radio pioneers who never lost their appeal. Vallee was credited with introducing Eddie Cantor to radio audiences. Bing Crosby starred for ten years on the "Kraft Music Hall," beginning in 1936.

Stars soon developed their own loyal followings; fans wrote them, saw every movie they were in, and collected their photographs. Teenage girls fainted in the presence of male crooners. Boys developed crushes on the female singers. Radio fan magazines were read from cover to cover.

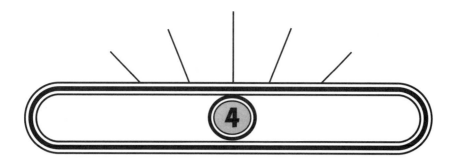

"Hello Again, This Is Jack Benny"

Now cut that out!

JACK BENNY

The threat sounded real. "Your money or your life!" The victim was silent. "Come on. Hurry up!" urged the impatient thief. After an even longer silence, the victim finally responded in a voice tinged with annoyance. "I'm thinking it over!" The audience roared with laughter. They understood the dilemma facing the "cheapest man in America."

From 1932 to the early 1950s Jack Benny was radio's best-known personality. He revolutionized radio comedy. Instead of the unconnected gags and puns that marked other programs, Benny created a continuing radio image for himself and his "gang" that focused on the entire cast and not just the star. Due largely to his success, other comedians changed their approach, so by 1937 radio comedy downplayed the old vaudeville techniques and developed its own unique style.

Jack Benny did not enter show business as a comedian. In fact, he did not enter it as Jack Benny. He was born Benjamin Kubelsky on February 14, 1894, the son of immigrant Jewish parents from Lithuania. Unlike other Jewish comedians, who were raised in large city ghetto slums like New York's Lower East Side, Benny grew up in Waukegan, Illinois, where his father operated a men's clothing store. He gained a lifelong love of music from his mother, who played the piano. When Benny was six his father bought him a small violin and paid for lessons. His father's dream was for his talented son to become a world-famous musician. When the boy's skills began to exceed the capability of local teachers, his parents sent him weekly to Chicago for private lessons with Professor Hugo Kortschak of the Chicago School of Music. While Benny may have liked music, he disliked the tedious practice sessions that his parents enforced. But, as he later wrote, he "hated school and homework even more."

His educational career ended during his first year of high school. He was continually truant and when he did attend school he often just talked and joked in class. Yet he excelled with his music and played in local orchestras. At age seventeen he got a job playing in the pit orchestra of the Barrison Theatre, one of the two vaudeville houses in Waukegan. From that moment he was hooked on show business. In 1911, when the young Marx brothers were playing at the theater, Benny was offered a job on the vaudeville circuit with the act. His father, still hoping his son would follow a more classical career, would not allow it.

But a year later, when the Barrison Theatre closed, his parents allowed him to go on tour with Cora Salisbury, the theater's piano player. Their act, "Salisbury and Kubelsky—From Grand Opera to Ragtime" opened at the Majestic Theater in Gary, Indiana, with Benny dressed in a tuxedo from his father's shop. His first name change occurred a few weeks later, when an attorney for the noted violinist Jan Kubelik threatened to sue Benny for appropriating the violinist's name! Rather than explain that Kubelsky was indeed his legal name,

Benny adopted a stage name. He became Ben K. Benny. In 1913 the act broke up when Miss Salisbury had to return home to tend to her ailing mother.

Benny next teamed up with pianist Lyman Woods. While Salisbury and Kubelsky had taken music seriously, Bennie and Woods, to the delight of the audiences, inserted humor into their act.

Their partnership broke up in 1918 when Benny enlisted in the United States Navy. The only action he saw during World War I was onstage as an actor and entertainer in navy camp shows, but he always credited his navy career with turning him from music to comedy. He quickly discovered that audiences preferred his monologues and jokes to his violin playing. From that point on, the violin became only a prop.

When he was discharged from the navy, Benny went back to vaudeville as "Ben K. Benny—Fiddle Funology." Perfecting the techniques he had developed in the navy shows, he displayed a suave stage presence that audiences found appealing. Staying away from the weird costumes and wild antics of other entertainers, he projected an image of sophistication. A second name change occurred when he realized that his stage name was similar to that of a well-known vaudeville star, Ben Bernie. Taking the name Jack, with which sailors of the time addressed one another, the former Benjamin Kubelsky and Ben K. Benny became Jack Benny.

He moved with ease to the top of the vaudeville world. His classy manner and easy wit pleased audiences and theater owners. In 1924 he starred at the Palace in New York and in 1926 appeared on the Broadway stage in "Great Temptations."

In 1927 he married Sadie Marks. He had actually met her years earlier, when Sadie was a girl of thirteen and he was on the road with his act. Zeppo, one of the Marx brothers, to whom Sadie was related, took Jack to a Passover seder at the Marks home in Vancouver, Canada. They did not see each other again until 1926, when they were separately invited for dinner by Sadie's older sister, Babe, and her husband, a vaudevillian Benny knew. Benny was taken with the beautiful young woman and her sense of humor and began visiting her at her place of work, the hosiery counter at Hollywood's May Company department store. Jokes about the May Company and Babe became standard fare on later Benny radio shows.

In 1928 Benny was hired as master of ceremonies at the Palace and his national reputation as a comedian and monologuist grew.

His first radio appearance was as a guest on the "Ed Sullivan Show" in New York on March 29, 1932. Benny was nervous. Today, his opening on that show seems rather pointless. "Ladies and gentlemen, this is Jack Benny talking. There will be a slight pause while you say, 'Who cares?' " Nonetheless, someone thought he had radio potential and offered him a contract to star on the "Canada Dry Ginger Ale Program" on NBC. The first program was broadcast on May 2, 1932. By the fourth program he varied the opening from the Sullivan show. "Hello, somebody. This is Jack Benny talking. There will be a slight pause while you say, 'What of it?' After all, I know your feelings, folks, I used to listen in myself."

He hired a well-known gag writer to provide him with material and began his trademark inclusion of commercials in the program itself, something other radio comedians had not yet attempted. On the first program he inserted the name of his sponsor into an old vaudeville one-liner from Prohibition days. "Her father drank everything in the United States and then went up north to drink Canada Dry." The sponsor was not quite ready for such daring and dropped Jack Benny at the end of the year's contract.

His next sponsor was General Motors's Chevrolet division. His introduction demonstrated the effort to turn his radio personality into that of a show-off. "Hello again. This is Gentleman Jack talking . . . America's representative youth . . . and unless I am mistaken, the Beau Brummell of the air. . . ." The program's main writer quickly saw the benefit of using other cast members to highlight Benny's radio characteristics, which soon evolved into stinginess and vanity. In *Radio Comedy* Arthur Wertheim notes that "instead of jokes stemming exclusively from the star comedian, the cast—the 'gang' as they came to be known—got laughs by picking on Benny, who became the butt of innumerable jests."

It was during this period that the Jack Benny "gang" was established. Most of the cast remained on the program for years as permanent members of a radio family. Jack's wife, Sadie, drafted into the role of Mary Livingstone, was an instant hit. She later legally changed her name. Forever more even her husband knew her only by her radio identity. There were several male singers over the years, each playing the similar role of a dim-witted complainer. The first was Frank Parker, who held the role for a few years. The person most associated with the role was Dennis Day, who joined the program in 1939.

The other permanent members of the gang were Phil Harris, the orchestra leader, who never ceased to annoy Benny with his loud voice, girl chasing, and hard drinking. His flip "Hiya, Jackson" or a chorus of his snappy trademark song, "That's What I Like about the South," usually preceded his opening lines on the show. Eddie Anderson played the role of Benny's valet, Rochester. At a time when few African Americans had opportunities to succeed in radio, Anderson's key role on Jack Benny's show made him a highly popular star. Anderson, whose parents had also been in show business, was a successful nightclub entertainer who frequently appeared at New York's famed Cotton Club. His unique, gravelly, sometimes high-pitched voice was instantly recognizable.

His portrayal of Rochester was stereotyped at first—drinking, gambling, happy-go-lucky. African Americans, although wanting to see Anderson succeed, were not at all pleased with Rochester's characterization. As the program developed, the stereotypes disappeared and the Rochester role grew. Although he remained Benny's valet, he

Jack Benny entertains troops during World War II. With him is his long-time announcer, Don Wilson. *Special Collections Department, University Research Library, UCLA.*

never was afraid of his boss. One of the delights of the program was Rochester's continual impertinence toward Benny.

> BENNY: Rochester, answer the door.
> ROCHESTER: Boss, you're nearer to it than I am.

Perhaps the best known of the supporting cast members was Mel Blanc, the man of a thousand voices. In the movies, he was the voice of Bugs

Bunny and Porky Pig, and on the "Jack Benny Show" he played a number of parts, including the sound of Benny's sputtering antique Maxwell automobile, a parrot, a polar bear named Carmichael, and Sy, the wayward Mexican, a man of few words, with an exaggerated Mexican accent.

> "You are the Tijuana Strings?"
> "Si."
> "I take it you are all from Tijuana?"
> "Si."
> "What is your name?"
> "Sy."
> "Sy?"
> "Si."

Or, the following variation.

> "Excuse me, sir, are you waiting for this train?"
> "Si."
> "A relative?"
> "Si."
> "What's your name?"
> "Sy."
> "Sy?"
> "Si."
> "This relative you're waiting for—is it a woman?"
> "Si."
> "Your sister?"
> "Si."
> "What's her name?"
> "Sue."
> "Sue?"
> "Si."
> "Does she work?"
> "Si."
> "Does she have a regular job?"

"Si."

"What does she do?"

"Sew."

"Sew?"

"Si."

No line broke up studio audiences more than one that frequently appeared in another railroad-station scene. Mel Blanc as a train announcer, pronouncing each word slowly and distinctly in a booming voice, called out, "Train leaving on track five for Anaheim, Azusa, and Cuc . . . amonga." In the mid-1930s these three cities were virtually unknown outside a thirty-mile radius of Los Angeles. Mel Blanc made them as well-known as New York and Boston. For some unexplained reason audiences could not control their laughter when they heard these cities announced. And the longer the pause between *Cuc* and *amonga*, the more prolonged the laughter.

Another of Mel Blanc's characters was Benny's long-suffering violin teacher, Professor LeBlanc. In real life Benny was an accomplished and serious violinist. On the radio he played an egotistical, vain, and unbearable musician. Poor Professor LeBlanc usually accompanied Benny's scale exercises with a rhyming insult, which his student never seemed to hear: "Make the notes a little thinner. / I don't want to lose my dinner." Or "What a pain your fiddle brings on. / How I wish it had no strings on."

Early in his radio career Benny perfected the successful formula for a weekly radio program. At a time when other comedians were running out of their old vaudeville jokes, Benny discovered a nearly inexhaustible source of material. He introduced skits based on popular books and movies and on his own fictional life outside of the broadcast. "Our sketches were the first real satires in radio," Benny later recounted.

While the audience and the gang easily recognized his faults, Benny's radio personality never admitted to any. His eyes were perfect

A 1942 broadcast of a Jack Benny program. *Left to right:* Jack Benny, Mary Livingstone, Don Wilson, and Dennis Day. Other cast members await their cues to speak. *Special Collections Department, University Research Library, UCLA.*

baby blue, his age a never-ending thirty-nine, and his violin playing of concert-hall excellence. And that was what appealed to the radio audience. "Funny things happen to us all the time," Benny explained. "The comedian or comedy writer must be alert to these, remember them, and invent variations on them."

Benny once said, "The show itself is the important thing. As long as people think the show is funny it doesn't matter to me who gets the punch lines." Over the years audiences found it particularly funny whenever he talked about his tightness with a dollar. Before long, the name of Jack Benny became synonymous with stinginess and conceit, although his radio character never seemed to realize how others saw him.

PROFESSOR LEBLANC: Monsieur Benny, you 'aven't pay me for your violin lesson today.

BENNY: Ah, yes, how thoughtless of me, Professor. Have a chair.

PROFESSOR LEBLANC: I had a chair last time. Today I want the money.

Jack Benny recognized that radio listeners were unlike vaudeville audiences. People at home had to use their imaginations. Grimaces, offbeat clothes, and gestures had no effect on the families gathered around the radios in their living rooms. Words, intonations, and, as Benny discovered, silence, were the powerful tools radio stars had to master successfully to paint pictures in the listeners' minds. "Timing is not so much knowing when to speak," Benny once said, "but when to pause. Timing is pauses."

Certain catchphrases, uniquely spoken, became verbal symbols of Benny's character. A long, drawn out "Well!" or a thoughtful "Hmm" or a sharp "Now cut that out!" instantly told the listener what was happening. "Benny could say more with a simple 'Hmm,' " notes John Dunning in *Tune In Yesterday*, "than many comedians could say in a page of script."

Over time, listeners accepted Benny and his gang as their own family. Each had his or her own faults, habits, and distinct personality. Even the band members were not immune, and the image of them as heavy drinkers, sloppy dressers, and incompetent musicians was routinely accepted.

Each of Benny's shows was skillfully crafted down to the last word. After the first year, the programs generally followed a similar schedule. The program would open with seasonal banter among the gang, then switch to discussion about problems in arranging that week's sketch. A song by Dennis Day and a "surprise" commercial by Don Wilson rounded out the second section. Finally, there would be a short sketch, which usually featured a name guest star. A team of expert writers

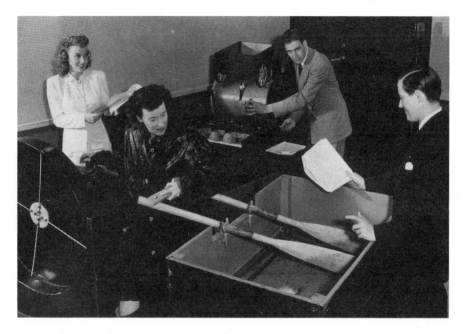

Using unsophisticated "tools," sound effects experts made radio dramas come alive. Here an NBC sound effects crew adds realism to a program. *American Library of Radio and Television, Thousand Oaks Library.*

toiled under Benny's direction to produce each show. "Playing comedy," Benny said, "is often as delicate an operation as taking apart the springs and wheels of a fine Swiss watch and putting them together again."

The writers created one of the best-known "feuds" in broadcasting. The long-running gag, which many listeners believed was true, pitted Benny against another star comedian, Fred Allen. The idea for a feud began when Allen had a ten-year-old child prodigy play a violin solo on his program. When the boy finished playing, Allen added, "After hearing you play, I think Jack should hang his head in shame." On Benny's next show, Jack accused Allen, a former juggler, of being tone-deaf from being hit on the head too often with falling clubs. Both comedians' writers saw the endless possibilities and met to plan the continuing feud.

Over the years, each appeared on the other's show, and gags about the feud filled the airtime of both Benny and Allen. In comparing himself to Allen on one broadcast, Jack said, "I am an actor, first, last, and always." To which Mary Livingstone, quickly deflating his ego, quipped, "You're a ham, baked, boiled, or fried!" When Benny's home city of Waukegan, Illinois, actually named a junior high school after him, the mayor planted a tree in honor of the occasion. Fred Allen could not stand idly by. "How can they expect the tree to live in Waukegan when the sap is in Hollywood?"

In truth, the two men were friends who greatly respected each other's work. In a moment of seriousness, Fred Allen spoke about his friend Jack. "Jack Benny is the best-liked actor in show business. He is the only comedian I know who dies laughing at all of the other comedians. He is my favorite comedian." Benny, in fact, was not a naturally witty person like Ed Wynn or Fred Allen. On one appearance on Fred Allen's show, when the ad-libs apparently caught Benny off guard, he humorously retorted, "You wouldn't talk to me like that if my writers were here!"

Perhaps the best example of the importance of timing in radio comedy is Jack Benny's classic routine "Your Money or Your Life." The writers were stumped: They could not think of a way for Benny to respond to the robber. One writer began nagging a second, who just sat quietly without responding. After a while, somewhat annoyed, the silent writer yelled, "Stop nagging, I'm thinking it over!" That was it. When Benny read it on the air after a suspenseful pause, the radio skit became part of broadcasting history.

Over the years Benny created a self-contained world with which his listeners could identify. The cast, the situations, the old Maxwell automobile, and especially Benny's radio personality were familiar, instantly recognizable, and welcome. "On the air I have everybody's faults," Jack Benny once said. "All listeners know someone who is a tightwad, show-off, or something of that sort. Then in their minds I become a real character."

For most of his radio career, from 1932 to 1955, Jack Benny occupied the same time period on the NBC network, Sunday nights from seven to seven-thirty. Unlike today, when few television programs are totally sponsored by one company, radio programs of the 1930s and 1940s were usually one-sponsor shows. His first sponsors, Canada Dry, Chevrolet, and General Tire, lasted only a year each. They did not seem to appreciate the unorthodox kidding about their products on the air and the way in which Benny and his announcer humorously made commercials part of the programs.

The next sponsor viewed Jack Benny much differently—as the world's most successful salesman. From 1934 to 1948, the name of Jack Benny was tied inseparably to one product of the General Foods Corporation: Jell-O. Jell-O was a new product in 1934; it was also one poorly received by consumers. As if by magic, sales of this almost unknown product skyrocketed beyond belief once Jack Benny began advertising it.

The program began with "Jell-O again, this is Jack Benny." Then, aided by longtime announcer Don Wilson, references to the dessert and its six delicious flavors would creep in (almost) unexpectedly in the middle of the program.

> WILSON: I shopped around until I found a half dozen neckties, each one corresponding to a different flavor of Jell-O, you know, strawberry, raspberry, cherry, orange, lemon, and lime.

Or:

> MARY: Oh, Wilson, what do you think I ought to get my mother? She's sixty-four years old and don't like spinach.
> JACK: Here it comes, folks.

WILSON: Get her some Jell-O, in all six delicious flavors and she'll find it's twice as rich as last Christmas.

MARY: Gee, that fits right into my budget.

Ed Wynn once paid Jack Benny the highest compliment one comedian could give another. He said Jack Benny was "the world's finest comedian—comedian meaning a man who says things funny, as opposed to a comic, who says funny things."

Wave the Flag for Hudson High

Plunk your magic twanger, Froggy!

SMILIN' ED McCONNELL

Late-afternoon and Saturday-morning radio programs were for kids. The first programs specifically for children were story times. Fifteen- or thirty-minute programs like "The Lady Next Door" or "The Book-house Story Time" kept children entertained with safe and simple retellings of familiar fairy tales while mothers prepared dinner.

Like early adult programs, the first children's shows were uncomplicated. Just as adult programming during the depression of the 1930s leaned toward lighthearted comedies, children's shows emphasized fantasy and escapism. A program host, usually called the story lady, if a woman, or Uncle if a man, would read stories over the air. "Salty Sam" on CBS and "The Singing Story Lady" on NBC expanded programming by adding music, sound effects, and actors to provide dramatic enactments of familiar and original stories. Many considered radio a bad influence on children, so helpful hints about safety or health were sometimes added to programs to make parents happy.

One of the earliest children's-program personalities was Ireene Wicker, "The Singing Story Lady," whose program began in 1932 over the NBC Blue Network. Her soft, pleasant voice and choice of stories appealed to children. Each week, kids eagerly awaited the program's opening lines:

> For stories true from history
> and fairy tales and mystery:
> So come along on wings of song.
> Oh, come to storyland with me.

Each evening the time slot from five to six o'clock on the major networks was filled with a number of "singing lady" competitors. Most programs aired three days a week for fifteen minutes each. "Salty Sam" was followed by "The Lone Wolf Tribe" on CBS, while Paul Wing, "The Story Man," appeared on NBC.

The classic children's show, the one by which all others were judged, was "Let's Pretend," which ran for twenty-three years beginning in 1939. Under the loving direction of Nila Mack, who personally wrote most of the scripts, the weekly program was performed in front of a live audience of children.

For the first few years, CBS carefully guarded the program from commercial sponsorship in order to maintain a respected image for the show. But pressure from would-be sponsors was too great, and the program became forever associated with Cream of Wheat cereal. At the start of each program, to the cheers of the studio audience, the cast sang one of the most popular commercials on radio.

> Cream of Wheat is so good to eat
> That we have it every day.

We sing this song, it will make us strong
And it makes us shout "Hooray!"

It's good for growing babies
And grown-ups too to eat.
For all the family's breakfast
You can't beat Cream of Wheat!

Hosting the program was Uncle Bill, who would greet young listeners
with a booming, "Hello, pretenders." The studio audience would respond with an equally rousing, "Hello, Bill." "How do we travel to
'Let's Pretend'?" Bill would then ask. A young cast member would
respond by naming a means of transportation that just happened to
relate to that week's chosen story. "Why don't we go on a railroad
train?" a young voice would ask. Then Bill would shout, "All aboard
for 'Let's Pretend,' Rumpelstiltskin, and points east!" and that week's
story would begin. Each week children were treated to perfectly
scripted fairy tales or original stories presented by child and adult
actors.

While on "Let's Pretend" Uncle Bill and the cast set a high standard for children's programming, other "uncles" had programs of their
own, with varying degrees of quality. Beginning in 1928 and lasting
for over twenty years, Uncle Don's popular program was heard in the
eastern United States. His program consisted of songs, jokes, and
birthday announcements, interspersed with the Pledge of Allegiance
and large numbers of commercials.

Hello, little friends, hello.
Hello, nephews, nieces mine.
I'm glad to see you look so fine.
This is Uncle Don all set to go
With a meeting on the radio.

Uncle Don is remembered best in radio history for an event that probably never happened. After one program, the story goes, the microphone was left on as Uncle Don supposedly said, "There! I guess that will hold the little———s for another night!" The story circulated for years, to the amusement of everyone except Uncle Don.

> I'm Buster Brown and I live in a shoe
> This is my dog, Tige, and he lives in there, too.

Another popular show was "Smilin' Ed's Buster Brown Gang." Each Saturday morning, Smilin' Ed McConnell and his cast of fantasy characters entertained a live studio audience and those at home in front of their radios. Smilin' Ed would tell Froggy the Gremlin to plunk his magic twanger, and off they would go into an imaginary world of wonderfully dramatized stories, songs, and heavy doses of commercials:

> I got shoes, you got shoes
> Why, everybody's got to have shoes!
> And there's only one kind of shoes for me,
> Good old Buster Brown shoes!

Children loved these shows—and their parents bought the shoes. Parents preferred the fairy-tale programs to other, more sophisticated shows for young listeners. The new drama and adventure programs contained too much violence or "inappropriate" behavior to suit some parents, but soon they eclipsed the well-mannered, "white-gloved" story ladies in popularity.

Many of the new programs had their origins in popular newspaper comic strips. "Little Orphan Annie," "Buck Rogers," and "Jack Armstrong" were among the earliest to make the leap from print to air and bring favorite characters to life. Along with adventure came advertising geared specifically to young listeners. "Say, do you want to be the envy of every boy and girl in your neighborhood?" the announcer would ask. As eager children at home listened intently, he would go on to describe at length the benefits of owning a unique, luminous dragon's-eye ring just like the one used in the program. All a young listener had to do was send a Wheaties box top and ten cents to Jack Armstrong, Minneapolis, Minnesota. Depending on the current adventure, the premium could be a Hike-O-Meter or a Jack Armstrong Norden bombsight (very popular during World War II).

Wheaties cereal, a product of General Mills, was not only the sponsor of the Jack Armstrong program but in many ways an integral part of the daily fifteen-minute program. The two were inseparable to listeners. Jack was a student at Hudson High, and every program began with a choral tribute to Hudson and a subtle hint that the program was sponsored by Wheaties, the "breakfast of champions."

> Wave the flag for Hudson High, boys.
> Show them how we stand.
> Ever shall our team be champions
> Known throughout the land!

Jack's adventures spanned the globe. Whether trapped in the Cave of the Mummies or chased by spies in Manila, Jack and his friends outwitted the evildoers every time, but not without creating some nervousness among the listeners. Jack never forgot to do the right thing no matter what danger he was in, and he always managed to finish his homework!

Each program ended with the musical praises of Wheaties.

> Have you tried Wheaties?
> They're whole wheat with all of the bran.
> Won't you try Wheaties?
> For wheat is the best food of man!

They're crispy and crunchy the whole year through.
Jack Armstrong never tires of them
And neither will you.
So, just buy Wheaties
The best breakfast food in the land!

Unlike Jack Armstrong, Tom Mix was a real live adventurer. Before becoming a well-known movie star he had been a rodeo star and a soldier who accompanied Theodore Roosevelt as a Rough Rider in the Spanish-American War.

The radio program based on his exploits became an early favorite. For fifteen minutes, five days a week, the continuing saga kept listeners glued to their radios.

The real Tom Mix did not appear on the show; his role was played by an actor. The programs were filled with murder, mystery, and adventure. As on many such shows, other cast members were always at the hero's side, sometimes to help, sometimes to confuse, and sometimes just to provide comic relief. Tom Mix was ably assisted by two young people, Jimmy and Jane, who helped listeners identify with the program. The Old Wrangler introduced the action. "Howdy, straight-shooters, howdy!" And everyone knew Tony the Wonder Horse.

Of course, there was always a word from the sponsor. In Tom Mix's case, a singing commercial for Shredded Ralston cereal opened each program.

Shredded Ralston for your breakfast.
Start the day off shining bright.
Gives you lots of cowboy energy
With a flavor that's just right.
It's delicious and nutritious,
Bite-size and ready to eat.
Take a tip from Tom.
Shredded Ralston can't be beat!

It sometimes seemed that American kids ate nothing but breakfast cereals during the 1930s and 1940s. Depending on program loyalty of the moment, mothers were nagged to buy a particular cereal, which soon made way for yet another brand. But the cereals didn't really matter—only the tops of the boxes were important to young listeners, since cereal-manufacturer sponsors required box tops to be mailed in for premiums. Tom Mix offered a great selection of prizes, ranging from rocket parachutes and whistling badges to coded comic books, each requiring that a separate Shredded Ralston box top and ten cents in coin be mailed to Ralston, Checkerboard Square, Saint Louis, Missouri.

> Who's that little chatterbox?
> The one with pretty auburn locks.
> Who can it be?
> It's Little Orphan Annie!

Annie was probably the best salesperson on radio. Her Ovaltine premiums were popular with listeners and countless jars of the chocolate syrup were bought strictly for the inner seal that had to be sent in for a decoder ring or two-in-one mug.

"Little Orphan Annie" was the first children's program to be presented in serial format. Beginning in 1931, the program was heard five days a week for fifteen minutes each day. Other programs adopted the same schedule and the afternoons were filled with fifteen-minute "chapters" competing for listeners over the different networks. Each program developed its own loyal audience.

Imagine yourself at home on a Wednesday afternoon in 1939. Mother is in the kitchen preparing dinner. You are sitting on the living room floor in front of the family radio. (Most homes had only one radio for everyone to share.) You begin turning the dial. It's five o'clock and you tune in "Dick Tracy" on the local NBC station. At five-fifteen, it's over to the Blue Network for "Terry and the Pirates." But at five-thirty you really have a problem. Usually, you listen to "Jack Armstrong" on NBC, but your friends have been telling you about a new program on the Blue Network, based on a comic strip you've been following in the newspaper, "Don Winslow of the Navy." (Winslow, a daring intelligence officer, fought evil for two seasons over the NBC Blue Network.) At five-forty-five there's no doubt for you—it's "Tom Mix." You've been listening to his adventures for years.

On the other hand, your friend across the street has begun listening to a new adventure story, "Captain Midnight," broadcast five days a week at the same time as "Tom Mix." The toll of a bell and the sound of a swooping airplane introduces each program as the announcer slowly shouts, "CAP-TAIN MIDNIGHT! Brought to you every day, Monday through Friday, by the makers of Ovaltine." The captain, a World War I hero, has been called back to fight villains who threaten the American way of life. His Secret Squadrons battle America's arch enemies over the airwaves.

Your friend is also a Secret Squadron member but never has to leave the chair in front of the radio to go into battle. Anyone could become a Secret Squadron member simply by having Mom buy a jar of Ovaltine. Then, by sending in the ever-popular jar seal and ten cents in coin, the young listener received a decoder badge allowing him or her (and several million other Ovaltine drinkers) to understand the secret messages broadcast at the end of each day's program.

The announcer introduced the series on the very first program. "In the air and on the ground you don't want to miss a single adventure. . . . Ovaltine is so downright good . . . and so good for you. Tell Mother you'd like to start drinking Ovaltine every single day and start listening to this swell new program." Each program ended in such a way that you just had to tune in the very next day to find out what happened. "What will be Captain Midnight's answer? Will he accept command of the Secret Squadron? Don't miss the exciting adventure tomorrow. Tune in same time, same station to CAP-TAIN MID-NIGHT! And don't forget to try Ovaltine this very night."

One of the most successful programs based on a comic strip was "Superman." Once changed into his Superman outfit, Clark Kent, mild-mannered reporter for the *Daily Planet*, just had to say "Up, up, and away!" and off he went into the sky. As in other radio shows, good acting, realistic sound effects, and imagination helped listeners of all ages visualize the impossible.

> Faster than a speeding bullet . . .
> More powerful than a locomotive . . .
> Able to leap tall buildings at a single bound.
> Look! Up in the sky!
> It's a bird!
> It's a plane!
> It's Superman!

Popeye entertained children, who first became acquainted with the stubborn sailor with the fractured vocabulary from his many movies and comics. But even the spinach-eating sailor had to change his diet to fit his sponsor.

> Wheatena's me diet.
> I ax ya ta try it.
> I'm Popeye the sailor man!

Other adventure stories were heard later in the evening or on the weekend. They attracted listeners young and old. "The Shadow" was perhaps the scariest of them all. To the background of eerie organ music, a sinister-sounding announcer welcomed listeners to the weekly broadcast: "Who knows what evil lurks in the hearts of men? The Shadow knows! Ha-ha-ha-ha."

Each week, Lamont Cranston transformed himself into an invisible champion, bringing assorted villains, traitors, and criminals to justice. "The weed of crime bears bitter fruit. Crime does not pay! The Shadow knows!"

One popular program, which ultimately led to an early television series, was "The Lone Ranger." Like other radio adventure stars, the Lone Ranger was a classic hero. He engaged in no frivolity, dressed immaculately, and spoke perfectly. He was brave, intelligent, courageous, and, as described by the longtime announcer, Fred Foy, "resourceful."

> Hi-yo, Silver!
> A fiery horse with the speed of light,
> A cloud of dust and a hearty Hi-yo, Silver!
> The Lone Ranger rides again!
> Return with us now to those thrilling days of yesteryear.
> From out of the past come the thundering hoofbeats of the great
>   horse, Silver.

Accompanied by his "faithful Indian companion, Tonto," the masked rider foiled evildoers and "led the fight for law and order in the early Western United States."

One of the best-loved programs for people of all ages portrayed the trials, loves, and tribulations of a typical American teenager. Each week, for fourteen years, the program began with the anguished cry of the lad's mother: "Hen-ree! Henry Aldrich!" The innocent response, in an easily recognizable cracking voice, was, "Coming, Mother." Poor Henry was always in trouble of one sort or another. But no matter how much trouble he was in, he never displayed any disrespect to his parents. Teenagers identified with Henry and his problems; parents tuned in to relive their own youths.

World War II brought the radio heroes together with a common

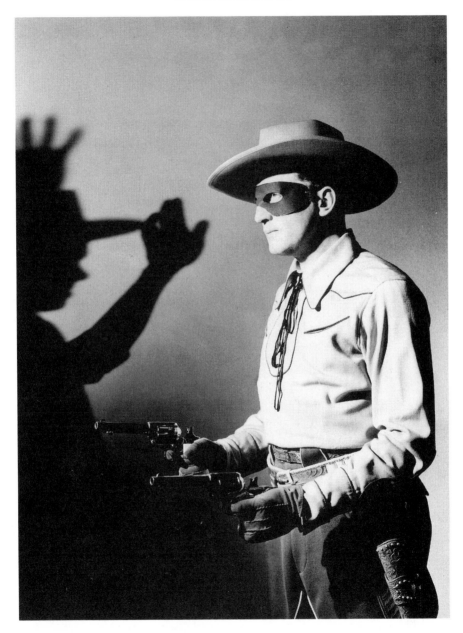

The Lone Ranger in a publicity shot taken in 1943. *Library of Congress.*

goal—to provide young people with patriotic role models and raise morale. "Terry and the Pirates" was the first children's program to openly speak up against fascism. This created some furor, since the United States was legally neutral until it entered the war in December 1941. Before the nation's entry into the war, radio programs were not permitted to portray acts of sabotage or spying within the country. Once the United States was at war, however, there was an almost instant change in programs and in advertising to reflect the patriotism of citizens whose nation was at war.

Quaker Oats pushed war-effort messages like "Uncle Sam wants you to eat to keep strong" while reminding listeners that their product was not rationed and was in plentiful supply. Children and adults heard messages on their favorite programs urging them to collect scrap metal, used bacon grease, and rubber, and to buy United States War Bonds. "Terry and the Pirates" concluded each program during the war with a special message to kids:

> Paper is a mighty weapon.
> Haul it in, keep smartly steppin'.
> Turn in every scrap you can
> To lick the Nazis and Japan.

In 1943, Dick Tracy led his young listeners in a special pledge:

> I pledge:
> To save water, gas, and electricity.
> To save fuel oil and coal.
> To save my clothes.
> To save Mom's furniture.
> To save my playthings.

Hop Harrigan, "America's ace of the airways," kept children on the edge of their chairs with his high-flying wartime adventures. The listeners, far from the battlefields of Europe and the Pacific, felt a part of the war through the always-victorious escapades of Hop and his friends.

Children's programs helped young people cope with the stresses of World War II. With fathers fighting overseas and mothers working double shifts in defense plants, children welcomed the reassurance they received from their favorite radio shows.

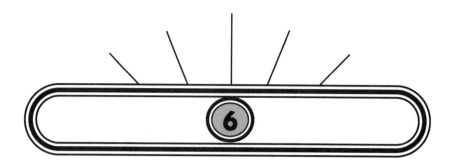

"Sold, American!"

The home is a sacred place and whatever
enters the home should be invited.

PRINTER'S INK MAGAZINE

In the early days of radio it was not considered "proper" to sell products directly. Instead, companies relied on the goodwill generated by the sponsoring of programs that reflected "good taste." The only hint of commercialism was the sponsor's name, which appeared prominently in most shows' titles. Musical shows abounded. There were the "Clicquot Club Eskimos" and the "Browning King Orchestra." So nearly anonymous were these sponsors that many listeners did not know what Browning King manufactured (men's suits).

Gradually, the sponsor's name and accompanying sales message became an integral part of the program. "Relax and smile, for Goldy and Dusty, the Gold Dust Twins, are here to send their songs there and brighten the corner where you are. The Gold Dust Corporation, manufacturers of Gold Dust Powder, engages the facilities of station WEAF. . . ."

Newspapers and magazines, the traditional mass media advertising vehicles, opposed radio advertising on the grounds that radio audiences would be forced to listen to it. In spite of this obviously self-serving view, it did not take long for sponsors to realize the major advantage of radio advertising over magazines: Radio produced a vast captive audience.

In the heady days of the 1920s, America was in a buying mood. New products appeared to make life more enjoyable, and workers, caught up in the desire to enjoy the "good life," could afford to buy. At the turn of the century manufacturers had simply relied on local distribution. As production techniques and automation increased America's production capacity, manufacturers needed ways to encourage consumers to buy. Advertising, first in print and later on radio, created increased consumer demand and allowed companies to sell their products to more widespread audiences. The fine art of advertising was born.

Advertising agencies quickly realized the potential of radio to distribute commercial messages to national audiences. It took some time for them to find the most effective ways to get these messages across, but advertisers learned which words and which types of delivery worked best for specific product types. Sound effects and music were introduced to highlight the messages and attract listeners' attention.

The agencies quickly discovered that the best way to market certain products was to create anxiety about personal appearance. Yet those were the days when it was unseemly to mention personal problems. Even toothpaste was considered too daring a product to talk about. People also did not think it polite to refer publicly to bad breath. The Lambert Company decided to push sales of its new Listerine mouthwash by promoting it as a cure for a respectable-sounding ailment called halitosis. Sales quickly skyrocketed.

The networks and the advertising agencies developed a special working relationship, which shaped American broadcasting. The sale of airtime gave networks money with which to fill the broadcast day with improved, more appealing programs. The agencies, in turn, controlled specific time slots for their respective sponsors. As the single source of network revenue, advertising agencies had immense influence over the networks. They decided on program content and hired on-air talent. Many of the nation's top-flight performers became part of a great sales force.

One of the many programs successfully created to market specific products was the revolutionary "Kraft Music Hall." In 1933, when most companies were trimming budgets because of the depression, the Kraft company was looking for a way to market its new Miracle Whip salad dressing. Tired of the type of musical programs then on the air, it wanted to create a program that relied more on imagination. They hoped listeners would also think creatively of their new product.

The opening of each show created the image of gold curtains parting while a full orchestra rose on an immense elevator stage to the strains of "Rhapsody in Blue." As an imaginary spotlight lit the stage, the famous conductor Paul Whiteman strode into view. Only the applause of the live audience and the sounds of the music were real, since the program was broadcast from a typically unglamorous studio. Radio listeners at home, by using their imaginations, made the program seem new and exciting.

The show was a huge success. Listeners enjoyed the quality entertainment; the sponsor enjoyed the increased sales. Kraft Foods's newsletter to its salespeople glowingly gushed, "And what a spot for the sensational new Kraft story—the story of Miracle Whip! The best hour, on the best radio night of the week, ten o'clock Eastern time, on Thursday night! Thursday is the night they stay home from the theater, when they neglect their bridge, when they 'shush' the visitors, to listen to the greatest galaxy of radio entertainment of the week."

There was no forgetting that the purpose of the program was to sell products. "The Kraft Music Hall," according to the newsletter, "has proven supreme advertising, carrying the Miracle Whip message into millions of homes throughout the country in a forceful, action-producing manner—best proved by the instantaneous success of Miracle Whip throughout the nation."

Other products were equally as successful. General Foods told its salespeople that the radio commercial "must put the story over and get the public to buy Jell-O, for after all, that is the acid test of any radio program."

In the days before national supermarket chains, Kraft realized the importance of radio as an aid to its own salesmen, who called upon thousands of small neighborhood stores: "Many grocery men are radio enthusiasts, listening in during the evening after they close the store." Other companies followed suit, urging their salespeople to use radio programs as sales aids.

One of the top shows in 1934 was "The Maxwell House Showboat." Typical of the advertiser involvement in programming of the time were the frequent coffee drinking and references to coffee on air by the stars. The second anniversary program of the "Showboat" was dedicated to the grocery trade. The president of the General Foods Corporation spoke directly to the listening audience. "We have been more than happy about the interest you've taken in the 'Showboat' and the way you have shown your appreciation by trying Maxwell House Coffee." Before the show, the General Foods sales force visited stores around the country and set up special displays. To radio listeners during the depression, advertising served to reassure everyone that in spite of economic troubles, America was still well. In its own way, the advertising of familiar, everyday products tended to bring people together.

Companies made heavy use of their radio stars to promote products. A bulletin from General Foods cheerfully informed salespeople,

Early radio stars heavily promoted their sponsors' products. Eddie Cantor poses with Chase and Sanborn's Coffee. *Special Collections Department, University Research Library, UCLA.*

"Don't think for a moment that Jack Benny stops selling Jell-O the minute he leaves the radio studio. To the contrary, he sells it all the time, no matter where he is appearing, and sells it hard." In 1935 a listener could send in three Jell-O box tops and receive a portrait of Jack Benny, suitably inscribed, "Jell-O again, Jack Benny." His picture appeared in newspaper and magazine advertisements and on in-store Jell-O displays. When he appeared live in theaters around the country, it was always as the "Star of the Jell-O program." So close was the identification of Benny with Jell-O that some listeners actually asked their grocers for "a box of strawberry Benny!"

During its sixteen years on the air, "Kraft Music Hall" presented listeners with a succession of stars, from Al Jolson to Bing Crosby. Each year, the sponsor, J. L. Kraft, appeared on the show with Bing Crosby to deliver a Christmas message as the Kraft employee choral group sang in the background. But no matter how popular the individual stars were, the sponsor was always king. The radio network had little influence. Once, Bing Crosby asked permission to tape a show in advance because of another commitment. The sponsor refused, insisted on a live performance, and actually filed suit against the popular entertainer.

While evening prime-time shows attracted advertisers of food and manufactured products, daytime programming offered other possibilities. Advertising for household products such as bleach, baking powder, flour, and soaps predominated. As early as 1929, certain product connections were obvious as Kraft and other food manufacturers sponsored daytime cooking programs designed for women listeners. As General Foods described that audience, "Most of the daytime shows are serial dramatizations, called soap operas. They are produced primarily for the vast army of American housewives, who, while busy with their household chores, find company and interest in the lives of other people."

First attempts to integrate commercials into the programming met with opposition from those who saw an erosion of the high-culture image so carefully cultivated by broadcasting's founders. In 1931 NBC's director of development Frank Arnold was piously moved to proclaim, "With the program once under way it is poor policy, as well as bad taste, to interject commercial announcements of a pronounced character between the entertainment numbers."

There were two types of programming—sustaining and sponsored. The sustaining shows were paid for by the networks themselves. Included were educational, religious, and cultural programs, which generally were not expensive to produce and had small listening audiences. The networks could point to them with pride, however, as examples of quality broadcasting. Some sustaining shows graduated to sponsored status, and although program content may not have changed, audience numbers grew as people perceived that if a sponsor was willing to spend money on a show, it must be more worthwhile. One radio news commentator wrote that even his friends thought more of him and of what he had to say when his program acquired a sponsor.

News programs were not high on the list of sponsor favorites until World War II. Sponsors preferred the light and popular shows featuring vaudeville stars, singers, and comedians, and the daytime soap operas.

By 1933 the advertising agency of J. Walter Thompson controlled nine popular NBC shows for its clients. So powerful were the agency executives that they had private telephone links with the studios from their offices blocks away.

When NBC opened its new Radio City complex in New York in 1933, each broadcast studio had its own special booth from which sponsors could view broadcasts in progress.

The legendary head of the Lord and Thomas agency was advertising pioneer Albert Lasker, whose early success with Pepsodent toothpaste's sponsorship of "Amos 'n' Andy" resulted in the tripling of sales for that brand. He also represented one of the most important radio sponsors of all time, the American Tobacco Company and its flamboyant head, George Washington Hill. Together, Hill and Lasker overturned all the accepted norms of the time and reinvented advertising.

George Washington Hill was a larger-than-life character whose sole reason for living seemed to be to sell his tobacco products. He wore outlandish hats and had himself driven daily to his office on New York's fashionable Fifth Avenue in a limousine decorated with pictures of Lucky Strike cigarette packages. Hill, who succeeded his father to the company presidency in 1926, was an early believer in radio as a selling medium. In 1928 he tested his belief by temporarily dropping all print advertising for Lucky Strike cigarettes and sponsoring a single radio show on NBC, the "Lucky Strike Dance Hour." Within two months, sales of the cigarette jumped 47 percent.

Although Lord and Thomas was responsible for the show, it was

Hill who dictated every aspect of the production and approved every song and entertainer before airtime. Hill was not subtle and used every aspect of his show to sell Luckies. Lasker once said of Hill, "The only purpose in life to him was to wake up, to eat, and to sleep so he'd have strength to sell more Lucky Strikes." Hill decided, for example, that the music should always be played in a simple upbeat tempo without the fancy arrangements common to other musical shows. Only popular tunes were heard on the program. He felt that people would feel more comfortable with familiar music and therefore feel more receptive to the commercial messages.

Hill had a flair for creating vivid and attention-grabbing advertising. While others viewed radio as an extension of older advertising methods, he saw the unique potential of radio to sell products. Radio had a voice of its own and Hill used it fully to his own advantage. His successes led other advertisers to quickly follow, and the world of aggressive radio advertising was born.

Hill's commercials were loud, brassy, and sometimes offensive. For a long time, CBS would not allow "undignified" commercials on the air. Yet, with the stock market crash of 1929, CBS found itself badly in need of funds. William Paley, the network chairman, invited George Washington Hill to a meeting and openly welcomed his brash advertising style to the network. In response to Paley's decision, listeners were able to hear "Spit is a horrid word" shouted at them between marching-band numbers on the Hill-sponsored "Cremo Military Band" program. The statement, which shocked many listeners, also boosted Cremo cigar sales dramatically. Without making a false statement, it led people to believe that all cigars except Hill's Cremo brand were "spit tipped," or moistened with a little spit to seal the tobacco wrapper. In fact, all cigars in Cremo's price category were machine made. CBS also permitted Hill to break the unwritten rule about not advertising prices over the air and blare that Cremo cigars, not made with spit, cost only five cents each.

Hill certainly had a way with words. His greatest successes came with his beloved Lucky Strike cigarettes. He had the ability to transform sophisticated or technical terms into language everyone could relate to. When looking for a slogan for Luckies, he discovered that the tobacco was actually heated to bring out the unique flavor. But how could he capitalize on that fact? He could say that the tobacco was cooked, but that did not sound very appetizing. Suddenly, he thought of a more appealing word: "It's toasted." Toasting conveyed a warm, tasty, and inviting image; the words became part of the Lucky Strike packaging and part of the commercials.

Hill explained his sales philosophy simply: "The wise advertiser must speak truthfully of the merit of the product. . . . no one in the tobacco business makes a profit on an initial sale. It's the repeat business that pays dividends."

In the 1920s there were millions of women smokers; they were considered modern and daring. But many more women did not smoke, and Hill saw them as an untapped market for Luckies. He accidently discovered the sales pitch with which to target women as he looked out of the window of a New York taxi one summer day. "There was a great big stout lady chewing gum . . . and there was a young lady and she had a very good figure and she was smoking. Right then and there it hit me. Reach for a Lucky instead of a sweet." Only the candy manufacturers objected as sales of Lucky Strike cigarettes to women increased.

During the Great Depression, with millions of Americans out of work, most industries experienced dramatic losses. Although the tobacco companies suffered, too, they were helped by increased radio advertising. The average smoker cut down on cigarette buying but never totally gave up smoking. The Richmond, Virginia, *Times Dispatch* described people's buying habits this way: "Even in hard times many people cut clothing and even food purchases before reducing their customary purchases of cigarettes and gasoline."

Johnny Roventini, a former hotel bellhop, was famous for his "Call-for-Philip-Morris" commercial. *American Library of Radio and Television, Thousand Oaks Library.*

In 1933 the Philip Morris Company discovered the new symbol for its cigarettes in the person of Johnny Roventini, a bellhop at the New Yorker Hotel. Johnny, who used to page hotel guests in the ornate lobby, became an overnight advertising sensation. His high-pitched B-flat voice was perfect for radio and his distinctive "Call for Philip Morris" was heard on radio commercials for years.

Hill sponsored a number of popular radio shows during the 1930s and 1940s, including "Information Please," Ben Bernie, Kay Kyser, and the later Jack Benny programs. His slogans and sound gimmicks became part of American folklore. In the early 1940s he abbreviated a successful slogan, Lucky Strike Means Fine Tobacco, to the initials LS/MFT. Then, to the background of a clacking telegraph key, an announcer repeated the initials and a further reminder that Luckies were "so round, so firm, so fully packed, so free and easy on the draw." LS/MFT was printed on the bottom of each Luckies package. Hill also employed two veteran tobacco auctioneers at the unheard of sum of twenty-five thousand dollars a year each to chant the melodic, rapid-fire auctioneer's pricing chant, which ended in exaggerated pronunciation of the words "Sold, American!"

Even World War II could not slow down Hill. In 1942 his purchasing director informed him that the company would have to change the color of the green circle on the Lucky Strike packages. For a while, Hill had been considering the idea himself, to make the package more appealing to women smokers. Now chromium, a key ingredient of the green ink, was needed for the production of tanks. "Green ink has gone to war just like the soldiers," the executive told Hill. Hill immediately saw the promotional value in the change of ink color, and his famous wartime slogan, Lucky Strike Green Has Gone to War, was born. Those words were as well-known during the war as Remember Pearl Harbor. Sales increased 38 percent.

George Washington Hill was not the only advertiser to combine patriotic fervor with good old-fashioned advertising. "General Foods is doing its part to build morale while at the same time building goodwill for the company and its products," the company proudly informed its employees. Americans listened to their radios constantly during the war, especially to news programming, which increased to over one-quarter of all available broadcast time. While many consumer products were not available or in short supply, companies continued advertising to keep product loyalty alive until the war was over. But many also substituted public service messages on behalf of the war effort in place of their usual commercials.

In 1930 a soft-spoken announcer had introduced "The General Electric Hour" by saying, "Good evening, ladies and gentlemen. This is the General Electric Program. . . ." Another popular program also began simply, "The Clicquot Club Eskimos! Summoned for your entertainment from their igloos in the frozen Northland by the makers of Clicquot Club Ginger Ale. Clicquot is spelled C-L-I-C-Q-U-O-T." No loud music or clever slogan jarred the listener. It took George Washington Hill and those who followed to change the way American business sold its wares on radio and, later, on television.

The Never-ending Story

The subject of love is something we could go on talking about for days and days.

BESS, "HILLTOP HOUSE,"
SEPTEMBER 21, 1939

The agony was wonderful. In program after program, characters lied, cheated, plotted, gossiped, advised, cried, and laughed. Every day, Monday through Friday, listeners tuned in for fifteen-minute doses of their favorite radio serial programs—the soap operas of the airwaves. James Thurber, the noted writer, once observed that "a soap opera is a kind of sandwich. Between thick slices of advertising, spread twelve minutes of dialogue, add predicament, villainy, and female suffering. . . . Throw in a dash of nobility, sprinkle with tears, season with organ music, cover with a rich announcer sauce, and serve five times a week."

The daytime serial programs began in the early 1930s and were targeted to a ready-made audience, the American housewife. In that

76

era before most women worked outside the home, the daytime broadcasting hours were devoted to the types of programming women would find useful and entertaining. Food shows, complete with recipe-repeating announcers, competed with programs sponsored by local stores, which told about the latest fashions or sales. To fill in the remaining daytime hours, radio stations had their announcers read short stories over the air. It did not take long before station managers assigned actors to portray characters. Listeners loved the innovation. So did sponsors of household products. Soon the afternoons revolved around the continuing stories, called serials, sponsored by soaps, detergents, cleansers, and bleaches. The soap opera was born.

It is difficult to assign the honor of the first radio soap to any one program. While "Amos 'n' Andy" and "The Rise of the Goldbergs" were broadcast on a daily schedule, they did not qualify as true soaps.

Radio performers read artfully from carefully prepared scripts. *Library of Congress.*

Real soap operas were ongoing stories, broadcast fifteen minutes a day, with continuing characters and story lines. They were supposed to be realistic accounts of people who led typical American lives. Most soap opera heroes and heroines were white, middle-class, and Protestant.

The characters, however, were far from typical. They experienced murder, marital problems, fatal illnesses, treason, corruption, deception, blindness, and the favorite ploy of soap writers—amnesia. Some characters experienced *all* these horrors during their tortured radio lives.

All this typical untypical misfortune took place in realistic settings. Small, fictitious towns in mid-America were favored by the writers, who placed the leading characters in familiar situations. Ma Perkins owned a lumberyard in Rushville Center. Just Plain Bill was a barber in Hartville. Papa David of "Life Can Be Beautiful," unusual among soap opera characters because he spoke with a Yiddish accent, owned a small bookstore in another typical rural town. "If the characters inhabit a small, average town where they own a Cape Cod cottage, mow their lawn, and drink endless cups of coffee even as does the audience," commented Edmonson and Rounds in *From Mary Noble to Mary Hartman,* "then it is easier for that audience to establish a connection with the characters and to believe that their emotions are genuine, their tears wet, and their problems worth solving."

And what problems! Listeners could count on a steady stream of programs during the day to keep them occupied with other people's misfortunes. When asked to comment on the reason listeners continued to tune in daily, Anne Hummert, the undisputed queen of soap opera writers, said, "Worry, for women, is entertainment." The stories were specially designed to move the action along in the slowest possible manner, sometimes stretching out a single day's events into years. If a listener left the country for a three-week vacation, upon returning she could pick up the story without any difficulty.

At one time Anne Hummert and her husband, Frank, had over thirty serials on the air. They did not invent the soap opera, but they turned it into a vast business. While the Hummerts developed the specific plots for each program, dozens of writers in their employ did the actual scripting. The Hummerts arranged the sponsorship for each series and contracted for the actors; all the networks had to do was provide the broadcast slots and collect the fees for the airtime. Other soap opera originators, like Elaine Carrington ("Pepper Young's Family," "When a Girl Marries") and Irna Phillips ("The Guiding Light," "Road of Life") worked in the same manner as the Hummerts, but no one approached the Hummerts in sheer quantity or style.

Their programs set the standard by which others were judged. Certain rules had to be followed in each broadcast. Actors had to carefully pronounce their words, without interrupting another character's lines, so that listeners could understand every word. Names of characters had to be constantly mentioned so that the audience could keep track of who was who. Likewise, the already slow-moving story lines were peppered with frequent plot summaries so that anyone missing a day (or a month) could quickly figure out what was happening. Music was carefully controlled to underscore the mood of the moment. With an almost uniform reliance on organ music, the soaps probably kept more organists employed than at any other time in history.

The soaps themselves were remarkably similar in content. Marital problems, sicknesses, and love predominated. While the plots and settings could have been interchanged, the main characters remained unique. Between ten-thirty and four-thirty the networks competed for listeners. In 1939 there were over sixty "women's serial" programs on the air. Among others, one could choose between the following programs at different times of the day:

| 10:30 | Just Plain Bill | (NBC) | Mary Martin | (Blue) |

11:30	Against the Storm	(NBC)	Big Sister	(CBS)
11:45	Guiding Light	(NBC)	Aunt Jenny	(CBS)
1:15	Ellen Randolph	(NBC)	Life Can Be Beautiful	(CBS)
4:30	Lorenzo Jones	(NBC)	Manhattan Mother	(CBS)
4:45	Young Widder Brown	(NBC)	Alice Blair	(Mutual)

And now, "Our Gal Sunday," the story of an orphan girl named Sunday from the little mining town of Silver Creek, Colorado, who in young womanhood married England's richest, most handsome lord, Lord Henry Brinthrope—the story that asks the question, can this girl from a mining town in the West find happiness as the wife of a wealthy and titled Englishman?

Each show had its own special introduction, usually accompanied by a familiar musical background. The introduction, read by an announcer, served at least two purposes: to repeat to listeners the program's original premise and to lead into the sponsor's first message of the program. Somehow, while the introduction provided a familiar beginning, over the years its message lost some of its truth. In the case of "Our Gal Sunday" there really was never any doubt about the positive relationship between husband and wife. In fact, one major theme that surfaced as a story line over the years was Lord Henry's almost insane jealousy of any man who showed interest in Sunday. The problems seemed to arise from outside the marriage. Sunday had continual strained relations with her stuffy aristocratic relatives, who often turned up at Lord Brinthrope's mansion, Black Swan Hall.

Each program ended with a polite invitation to return the next day. "What dramatic twist will the personal problems surrounding

Sunday take next? Be sure to listen tomorrow to the next episode of 'Our Gal Sunday.' "

> We give you now "Stella Dallas," a continuation on the air of the true-to-life story of mother love and sacrifice in which Stella Dallas saw her own beloved daughter, Laurel, marry into wealth and society, and realizing the differences in their tastes and world, went out of Laurel's life. These episodes in the later life of Stella Dallas are based on the famous novel of that name by Olive Higgins Prouty and are written by Frank and Anne Hummert.

Stella's "sacrifices" kept the program lurching from tragedy to tragedy for decades. At the heart of nearly all the stories was Stella's mission to keep her beloved "Lolly, Baby" happily married to her aristocratic husband, Dick Grosvenor, and on good terms with her husband's snobbish family, especially his mother.

In "Backstage Wife," Mary, a simple girl from Iowa, went to New York. There she became the secretary to Larry Noble, a Broadway star, whom she quickly married, in typical soap opera fashion: "The true-life story of Mary Noble, a sweet young girl from Iowa, who marries Broadway's most handsome actor, Larry Noble, dream sweetheart of a million other women, and the struggle she has to hold the love of her husband in the complicated web of backstage life."

Mary's life was not easy. Although many listeners would gladly have traded places with her to escape their humdrum, quiet lives, the story of Mary Noble showed how difficult it really was to be the wife of a famous man. Poor Mary was in almost constant battles with the succession of young actresses chasing after poor, naive Larry. She, however, heroine to millions of American women, never strayed from being the "noble" wife.

And then there was Helen Trent. She was a successful Hollywood dress designer who spent the best part of her two and one-half decades on radio looking for a husband and happiness. Lovers by the bushel proposed marriage to Helen, but her heart belonged to Gil Whitney, a handsome lawyer. Poor Helen experienced all life could offer, and by the end of the program's radio life she had been accused of murder, drugged, shot, and stabbed. Each program was introduced by a haunting melody hummed to the background of a strummed banjo.

> Once again we bring you the "Romance of Helen Trent," the real-life drama of Helen Trent, who, when life mocks her, breaks her hopes, dashes her against the rocks of despair, fights back bravely, successfully to prove what so many women long to prove in their own lives: that because a woman is thirty-five, and more, romance in life need not be over: that the romance of youth can extend into middle life, and even beyond.

The very last program tied twenty-seven years of broadcasting together with one simple and convenient twist. As Helen stood on her apartment balcony, despairing of her life and the fact that her beloved Gil had married another woman just a few years earlier, the balcony came loose and Helen fell to her death into the abyss below. At just that moment there was a knocking at the door and a voice could be heard shouting frantically, "Helen! Helen! It's Gil. Helen!" And that was that.

While nearly all soap operas were melodramatic, a few were built around other themes. Lorenzo Jones worked as a garage mechanic. He was also a less-than-successful inventor who came up with many an odd idea. "And now, smile a while with Lorenzo Jones and his wife, Belle." Lorenzo spent much of his time meddling in the lives of his neighbors. One memorable stretch of programming involved a long siege of amnesia, the common and convenient soap opera disease.

Marjorie Hannon and Hugh Studebaker, stars of the popular soap opera "Bachelor's Children." *Library of Congress.*

Some of the programs went through so many changes in plot, characters, and format that their original intent was no longer recognizable. "The Guiding Light" first appeared on the air in 1937 as the story of Rev. John Ruthledge and his family and friends. Throughout the show's early years, Irna Phillips, the program's originator and writer, inserted religious teachings as a way of defining her view of American life, particularly at Christmas and Easter, when the full fifteen minutes of the program were devoted to a sermon. As the years passed, the religious messages diminished in importance.

On "Hilltop House" listeners met a woman who ran an orphanage. The program was "dedicated to the women of America. The story of a woman who must choose between love and the career of raising other women's children." When that scenario grew tiresome, the writers shifted the main character's interests, while continuing the problems. "Can a stepmother successfully raise another woman's children? Colgate Tooth Powder presents the real-life story of Kay Fairchild, a stepmother who tries."

At the end of each program, an announcer (always a man) enticed listeners to return. "John has become moody, restless . . . has steadfastly refused to tell Gwen anything about his sister-in-law. . . . Was John wise to accept Bess's sincere advice? Should John risk his own happiness and Bess's to have Gwen's son? In just a moment we'll look ahead to tomorrow's chapter of 'Hilltop House.' "

There were many different twists in the arrangements of the stories. Some soaps just went on and on for years with a story line that hardly seemed to change. Others wove plots together, placing emphasis first on one, then another, over an extended time period. "Aunt Jenny's True Life Stories" was unique in that it completed a story in five chapters—one week of broadcasts. Each program was introduced by Aunt Jenny and her faithful announcer, Danny. "Here's Aunt Jenny to tell you another of her real-life stories." This technique made sure that listeners, even if they had had to miss the previous day's broadcast, knew what was happening. At the end of the broadcast, Danny usually offered the audience a "tease." "It seemed like an unsolvable tangle. What did they do next? You'll find out tomorrow."

Perhaps the two most durable and beloved soap operas of all were the Hummert creations "Just Plain Bill" and "Ma Perkins." The two main characters had much in common. Some critics said that Ma was nothing more than a female Bill. Both lived in small towns, Bill in Hartville, Ma in Rushville Center. Bill was a barber, Ma owned a lumberyard. They knew all their neighbors and could be relied upon by anyone for help and advice (even if not requested). Their stories centered around family life. Both were widowed with children who grew older and had children of their own. Ma's three children were John, later killed in World War II; Evey, a semisophisticated gossip; and Fay, a single parent whose husband had left her. Ma was so closely identified with her sponsor that eventually the program was simply introduced, "And now, Oxydol's own Ma Perkins."

Virginia Payne played Ma Perkins in each of the 7,065 broadcasts over a twenty-seven-year period. While she held the record for the most years in a single part, she was not untypical of the casts and crews of long-running soaps.

Listeners were loyal to their chosen programs. Even children, home from school for a few days because of a cold, got pulled into the stories. As the fifteen minutes came to an end, they eagerly hoped to stay home an extra day to accept the announcer's kind invitation:

Be sure to listen to "Big Sister" tomorrow.

*   *   *

Listen for "Just Plain Bill" on this station at this same time tomorrow. This is Roger Krupp saying good-bye for "Just Plain

Bill" and for the Whitehall Pharmaceutical Company, makers of Anacin and many other dependable, high-quality drug products.

*   *   *

How will this affect Helen? Listen for the "Romance of Helen Trent" tomorrow.

*   *   *

What will happen to these brothers? What dramatic twist will the personal problems surrounding Sunday take next? Be sure to listen tomorrow to the next episode of "Our Gal Sunday."

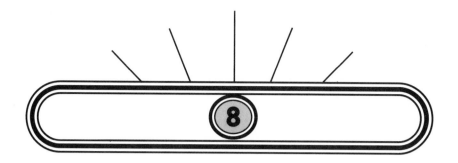

News While It Was News

Ah, there's good news tonight.

GABRIEL HEATTER

Today we turn on our radios or televisions and receive the latest news from around the world. We take it for granted. Using the airwaves to inform seems perfectly natural and expected. It was different in the early days of broadcasting. There were a few notable presentations of historic events, but no one realized the obvious implication of using radio as a public news medium. In 1920 station KDKA provided live returns for that year's presidential race between Warren G. Harding and James M. Cox. Listeners were fascinated. Two years later, the winner of that election, Harding, gave the first presidential address over radio as he dedicated a memorial in Baltimore to Francis Scott Key, the composer of the national anthem.

In 1924 the Democratic and Republican conventions were broadcast live for the first time. This was the beginning of the end for the smoke-filled-room style of choosing presidential candidates, where political deal makers controlled choices from behind closed doors. Throughout the country people now had front-row seats to the election process. When the chairman of Alabama's delegation to that year's Democratic convention rose to cast his vote, the entire nation heard his slow-paced, booming declaration, "ALA-BAM-AH casts twenty-four votes for Oscar W. Underwood." Underwood was quickly forgotten, but those words became a national joke. Radio had created its first catchphrase!

When Charles A. Lindbergh made his historic flight across the Atlantic in 1927, radio provided anxious Americans with nearly instant coverage of the pilot's progress. The bulletin that he had landed safely in France was received with joy and relief by millions of Americans. On his return, listeners throughout the United States felt as if they were experiencing the New York ticker tape welcome as NBC stationed announcers at points along the parade route to broadcast every detail. It was the first time that radio utilized multiple reporters to cover an event.

Using the lessons learned in covering Lindbergh's homecoming, radio provided listeners with in-depth coverage of the presidential inauguration of Herbert Hoover in 1929. That broadcast was heard by the largest radio audience up to that time. Still, news coverage was mainly limited to special events. Daily news, when a local station offered it, usually consisted of the reading of newspaper headlines by an announcer.

The first major network program devoted exclusively to news was "The March of Time," which began on CBS in 1931. For most of its twenty-four years on the air it was sponsored by *Time* magazine. Backed up by an in-studio orchestra, a distinguished cast of actors, and carefully researched sound effects, the program relied on the worldwide resources of the magazine to present dramatized versions of current events. The authoritative voice of announcer Westbrook van Voorhis added greatly to the effect. He ended each program segment with "Time marches on!" It may not have been pure and unbiased news, but listeners relied on the program for insight into important happenings.

For most of broadcasting's first decade, however, the newspaper remained the major source of news. Although newspapers at first welcomed radio's use of headlines as a way of selling more copies, publishers soon realized that radio offered serious competition. Advertisers discovered the immediate impact of selling their wares over radio and cut back spending on newspaper space. Coverage of the 1932 presidential election by both CBS and NBC was unacceptable to the newspapers. Even with late extra editions, the printed word could not compete with the immediate election results broadcast over radio. Thus began one of the most curious episodes in broadcasting history: the Press-Radio War.

Newspapers and radio networks received national and international news from press associations such as the Associated Press (AP) or United Press (UP). In 1933, under pressure from newspaper members, the press associations withdrew services from the radio networks, thereby depriving radio of its major news sources. In response, networks developed their own news services. At NBC a clever news editor read the newspapers looking for major stories and then telephoned for further details and information from people who were directly involved or mentioned in the reports. Many times his stories were more comprehensive than the original newspaper reports.

CBS organized the Columbia News Service, which consisted of bureaus in major cities such as Washington, New York, Chicago, and Los Angeles. In other cities, the news service relied on independent reporters who were not on the network payroll but were paid only if and when their services were required. In retaliation, the newspapers limited all mention of CBS programming in their daily radio listings.

Before matters escalated even further, a compromise of sorts was struck. Both parties agreed to the establishment of the Press-Radio

Bureau, responsible for producing radio news programs that satisfied the newspapers. Limits were set on the length and number of daily news programs that could be broadcast: Shows could not exceed five minutes each. The programs also had to be scheduled not to precede the release of morning or evening newspapers. At the end of each news broadcast the announcer had to repeat the following phrase: "For further details, consult your local newspaper." The agreement lasted only a short time. Radio was too big to control and began developing its own style of reporting.

By the mid-1930s CBS offered its network-affiliated stations three national news programs daily—two five-minute programs at noon and 4:30 P.M. and a fifteen-minute program at 11 P.M. Local stations continued to develop their own news broadcasts. Regional news networks that linked a small number of stations also became popular. In Boston, for example, WNAC linked together smaller New England stations to form the Yankee Network News Service. Each regional broadcast began with the words, "News while it is news: The Yankee Network News Service is on the air."

The power of radio to reach people and influence them was obvious. Using the medium correctly made the difference between success and failure for many political figures. Among those who used radio best was the thirty-second president of the United States, Franklin Delano Roosevelt. FDR was the first president to speak directly to the American people, which he did in a series of thirty "fireside chats" between 1933 and 1945. His unique speaking style, a balance of informality and authority, was perfect for radio. He quickly realized— as did his political opponents—that a president's political agenda could be furthered simply by speaking directly to the American people.

In a world that was changing by the moment, and in which those changes were being reported instantly by radio, someone needed to help the listening public make sense out of what was happening. The 1930s saw the creation of a new breed of on-air personality—the radio

President Franklin D. Roosevelt used the power of radio to boost the morale of Americans during World War II. *Franklin D. Roosevelt Library.*

news commentator. One of the first was H. V. Kaltenborn, who in 1922, as a reporter for the *Brooklyn Daily Eagle,* delivered radio's first editorial. In the 1930s, with the Great Depression in full bloom and the threat of war hanging over Europe, H. V. Kaltenborn was one of the most listened-to people in broadcasting. The announcer's introduction to his 1935 program, "Kaltenborn Edits the News," sheds some light on H. V.'s role: "What news means is even more important than the news itself. H. V. Kaltenborn—editor, author, dean of radio commentators—tells you what is in back of the headlines. Throughout his brilliant newspaper and radio career, he has had firsthand contact with the outstanding men and events of our time. You hear the voice of authority when 'Kaltenborn Edits the News.' "

For over two decades listeners looked forward to Kaltenborn's formal, rapid-fire delivery of his opinions about world events. Sometimes he personalized his presentations to make listeners feel more like active participants. During the Spanish Civil War he once reported on a battle that took place near the French border. From his vantage point, and with his microphone clearly picking up the sound of firing machine guns, he vividly described the ongoing battle to Americans snug in their peaceful homes. "We happen to be straight in the line of fire," he explained as the folks back home clearly heard the bullets whiz past his position.

Commentators presented their personal views on the day's happenings rather than an unbiased reading of the news. As a group, they were highly respected; as individuals they held widely differing political views. Drew Pearson, Raymond Gram Swing, Dorothy Thompson, Fulton Lewis, and Elmer Davis each had his or her own devoted following.

The first daily newscaster on radio was a swashbuckling journalist by the name of Floyd Gibbons. He was the very picture of a stereotypical war correspondent. Flamboyant, often drunk, he wore a patch over the eye that had been shot out as he covered a World War I battle. During his exciting career as a war correspondent he rode with Pancho Villa across the Mexican border and was aboard a ship torpedoed by a German submarine in the mid-Atlantic. In spite of his death-defying experiences, he proved to be overly brash as far as CBS and the sponsors were concerned. In 1930 he was permanently replaced by a worldly commentator of a different sort, Lowell Thomas.

Thomas was a well-known lecturer and author whose own adventures were just as exciting as the ones Gibbons experienced. Thomas made documentaries about his around-the-world trips, explored remotest Alaska, and reported on British General Allenby's entrance into Jerusalem during the First World War. Thomas was also credited with being the "discoverer" of the legendary British military leader of the Arabs, Lawrence of Arabia. Thomas was a master of description

Lowell Thomas, shown broadcasting over the NBC Blue Network. *American Library of Radio and Television, Thousand Oaks Library.*

and his conversational broadcasting style appealed to listeners. For decades people looked forward to Lowell Thomas's cheery greeting, "Good evening, everybody." He ended each fifteen-minute program on a note of continuity—"So long until tomorrow."

Charles A. Lindbergh twice accelerated the development of radio news. In 1927 his solo flight across the Atlantic demonstrated the power of radio to communicate news instantly to an anxious public. In 1932 the kidnapping of his baby captured the interests and emotions of people everywhere. Lowell Thomas somberly announced, "The world's most famous baby has been kidnapped and the attention of literally the whole world has been aroused." Newspaper reporters and radio commentators descended upon Hopewell, New Jersey, to cover the story. This second Lindbergh incident reinforced radio's unique quality as an instant information source and advanced the broadcasting careers of a number of radio commentators.

Boake Carter, who became a radio commentator in 1930, gained national attention for his continual on-site coverage of the Lindbergh kidnapping. Throughout the case, from the discovery of the baby's dead body to the arrest, trial, and execution of the man convicted of the kidnapping, Carter and his colleagues fed listeners a steady diet of news sprinkled generously with personal opinions and tough views on crime and punishment in America.

In contrast, Gabriel Heatter, another well-known commentator, broadcast his account of the kidnapping in a softer, more sympathetic style. When the execution was delayed, Heatter, without a script, spoke to the radio audience for fifty-five minutes about the case. His style and upbeat manner continued right on through World War II. "Ah, there's good news tonight," was his standard opening. He explained his philosophy once by saying, "Even when the news was grim, I tried to find a patch of blue or even a straw on which to hang real hope." The only break with that thinking was his opening at the end of World

War II when Hitler's death was announced: "Ah, Hitler is in hell tonight!"

Perhaps the most famous commentator of them all during the 1930s was a newspaper gossip columnist who started his career as a vaudeville dancer. Walter Winchell also covered the Lindbergh kidnapping. Shortly thereafter he was rewarded with his own network news show, a show like no other on radio. Speaking in a near-hysterical voice, Winchell, who unlike his colleagues had a limited education, opened each program with clipped urgency. "Good evening, Mr. and Mrs. North America and all the ships at sea!" He punctuated his stories with words like *Flash!* and the meaningless tapping of a telegraph key to enhance the image of urgency. His gossipy tidbits attracted many listeners.

Each of the well-known commentators developed a unique style and presentation. Edwin C. Hill explained his own successful formula in this way: "First I hit the audience with some topic which is both timely and of general interest, after which I tell about some amusing angle followed by a touch of sentiment or an emotional appeal and conclude with some intensely dramatic item." Some had specific political agendas. Father Charles Coughlin, a Roman Catholic priest, was a popular commentator who broadcast from his Church of the Little Flower in Michigan. He started out as a religious broadcaster but soon began championing right-wing political causes and religious intolerance, particularly against Jews. For a while his program was quite popular, as he seemed to fight against minority rights, President Roosevelt's economic policies, and American involvement in a war against Germany. His popularity dropped suddenly with the United States' entrance into World War II.

There were few women commentators during that period. Perhaps the best known was an overseas newspaper columnist, Dorothy Thompson. In 1936 she covered the presidential conventions for NBC and the next year began a weekly news commentary program on the same network. Other women who were heard on the networks were Mary Marvin Breckinridge and Betty Wason on CBS, Sigrid Schultz on Mutual, and Margaret Rupli and Helen Hiett on NBC. At a time when women broadcasters were mainly limited to programs with "women's" themes, network executives were afraid that listeners would not take their commentaries on world events seriously.

As radio news coverage of important events increased, broadcasters were limited by station bans on the use of recordings. Tape recorders had not yet been invented, but there was a cumbersome disk recording system that could capture the sounds of an event "by electrical transcription" for later broadcast. At a time when most stations did not employ news reporters, the use of recordings could provide news to stations and listeners who otherwise would have no direct news sources.

In 1937 a Chicago announcer, Herb Morrison, received permission from his station to conduct an experiment. Taking a recording system and a station engineer with him to Lakehurst, New Jersey, Morrison planned to record the routine landing of the German dirigible the *Hindenburg*. Then, by sending the disk back to Chicago on an airplane, he could demonstrate how this technique might help stations bring timely news from distant points to local listeners.

Morrison got more than he bargained for. Eight minutes into his description of the landing, the *Hindenburg* exploded. As flames devoured the huge craft, Herb Morrison continued talking into his open microphone. In an excited, almost hysterical voice, Morrison yelled to his engineer, "Get this, Charley! Get this, Charley! It's on fire!" Then, without a moment's pause, the shocked announcer continued his report. "It's crashing! Oh, my! Get out of the way, please. And the folks—oh, it's terrible! This is one of the worst catastrophes in the world. Oh, the humanity! All the passengers! All the people are screaming around here. . . ." Thirty-six people died in the crash; sixty-one survived.

Chicago station WLS broadcast the recording the next morning. Since WLS was an NBC affiliate, the recording was offered to the network. Breaking with its long-standing rule that permitted only live reporting, NBC broadcast the recording over the entire network. Herb Morrison's dramatic demonstration changed the sound of broadcast news. As World War II loomed ahead, radio was about to become a vital link between the people of the United States and developments abroad.

In 1930 CBS sent Cesar Saerchinger to London as its European director. His job was to look after the network's affairs in Europe. He arranged for noted European personalities to speak on the air and he himself broadcast when necessary. Even with direct broadcasts from Europe, the network still relied on H. V. Kaltenborn in New York for analysis of what Saerchinger reported. Two years later NBC sent Fred Bate to England with a similar assignment. NBC, perhaps feeling that the country to cover was Germany, also hired a second correspondent, Max Jordan, to report from Berlin. Saerchinger and Bate competed with each other as they scoured Europe for stories. Each had his share of "scoops," but it was Saerchinger who beat NBC with the love story of the century.

With the death of England's King George V in 1936, the throne passed to King Edward VIII. As the world looked on, Edward revealed his love for an American divorcée, Wallis Simpson. In accordance with British tradition, the king had to make a choice between his throne and his beloved Wallis. Through a contact at Buckingham Palace, Saerchinger learned what the king's final choice was and broke the story over CBS hours before Edward himself sat down before radio microphones to solemnly announce, "I tell you that I have found it impossible to carry the heavy burden of responsibility and to discharge my duties as king, as I would wish to do, without the help and support of the woman I love."

In the late 1930s, with World War II about to erupt, radio news finally came out of its shell to assume its unique role as a serious and respected journalism form. On the strength of one man's vision, a new age of broadcast journalism was about to begin.

"This . . . Is . . . London"

I, for one, do not believe that a people who have the world brought into their homes by a radio can remain indifferent to what happens in the world.

EDWARD R. MURROW

If any one individual can be said to represent broadcast journalism in the twentieth century, it is Edward R. Murrow. He was not trained as a journalist and never worked on a newspaper, yet by the end of World War II he was considered the world's greatest reporter.

He was born in North Carolina in 1908. When he was four years old the family moved to the state of Washington, where young Murrow went to school. He attended Washington State College, where he studied history and speech. During high school and college vacations he worked on timber crews in the forests of the Pacific Northwest. He once remarked, "I'm probably more proficient with an axe than I am with a typewriter."

From 1930 to 1935 he worked for several educational organizations. He was president of the National Student Federation and in 1932 became assistant director of the Institute of International Education. In both positions he traveled around the country and to Europe, making speeches, raising money, and getting a firsthand view of political and economic conditions. He was particularly concerned with the growing threat of war coming out of Germany.

In 1935 Murrow was offered the job of director of talks and education for CBS. This was a welcome opportunity. He was responsible for locating "experts" to speak on the air on timely topics. He did well in this position and in 1937, with events exploding across the Atlantic, CBS offered and Murrow quickly accepted the position of European director for CBS. Cesar Saerchinger had resigned from that post: He saw no future at all in broadcast news! It was, Murrow later admitted, "The most important decision of my life. . . . [It] gave me an opportunity to be in a front-row seat for some of the greatest news events in history."

At first, his new European assignment was a continuation of what he had been doing—arranging talks and lining up programs. Other people would actually do the broadcasting. The onrush of world events quickly turned the barely known, behind-the-scenes director into a public personality. One of the first things Murrow did was hire William L. Shirer, a well-known newspaper reporter and author, to assist with the logistics of covering Europe for CBS. They, in turn, relied on "stringers," reporters for American newspapers and wire services stationed throughout Europe, to do the actual on-air broadcasting of their stories. This haphazard way of presenting the news to American radio listeners ended in 1938 when Germany annexed its more-than-willing neighbor Austria in a move known as the *Anschluss*.

In March of 1938 Shirer was in Vienna, Austria, as the Nazis were poised to take over the city. Swastika flags fluttered high and joyous crowds milled in the streets. This was an important story, and Shirer was the only American radio reporter in the city, but the Nazis would not let him broadcast. Shirer immediately contacted Murrow, who was in Warsaw, Poland, arranging for a children's radio program.

Speaking cryptically to avoid his telephone connection being cut off by German censors, Shirer simply said, "The opposing team has just crossed the goal line." Murrow understood, but needed to be absolutely certain. "Are you sure?" he asked Shirer. "I'm paid to be sure" was the cocky response.

Murrow advised Shirer to fly at once to London, where he could broadcast to the American public firsthand impressions of what he had seen in Vienna. Murrow himself took the only route open to Vienna by flying to Berlin and there chartering a twenty-seven-seat Lufthansa plane, for one thousand dollars, to fly him to the Austrian capital. Murrow reached the city in time to witness the Nazi takeover.

The next day, American radio listeners heard the first of what soon became standard for international reporting, the news "roundup." With events breaking out all over the continent, Murrow lined up knowledgeable reporters in major European capitals, overcame tremendous technical difficulties, and set out to invent a new format for radio news. At eight P.M. Robert Trout in New York, who didn't then realize he was the world's first news anchor, called the reporters standing by in London, Rome, Paris, and Berlin. Each in turn described the events from the perspective of the country they were in. From Vienna, Murrow, in the first official broadcast of his career, provided Americans with a vivid look at what was happening. "They lift the right arm a little higher here than in Berlin, and the 'Heil Hitler' is said a little more loudly. . . . There's a certain air of expectancy about the city, everyone waiting and wondering where and at what time Herr Hitler will arrive. . . ."

Murrow realized the world was edging closer to war. Yet neither American network had European news staffs to cover the breaking stories. In quantity and quality CBS soon set the standard by which broadcast journalism would be judged. On his return to London, Murrow began assembling the most influential group of news reporters in history. He chose the best and brightest young reporters he could find for their abilities to communicate and analyze—not for the sounds of their voices. On a CBS News broadcast Murrow later explained, "I tried to concentrate on finding people who were young and knew what they were talking about, without bothering too much about diction. . . ."

Most of the fledgling radio reporters had wire-service experience; none had broadcast training. Larry LeSueur, Bill Downs, and Eric Sevareid came from United Press, as did two Rhodes scholars, Charles Collingwood and Howard K. Smith. Years later Collingwood recalled Murrow had told him he was hired because he "seemed literate enough and . . . had not been contaminated by print." Others were hired away from similar news positions. They all shared H. V. Kaltenborn's enthusiasm for news. The news, Kaltenborn had once said, had "interested me since most boys were playing with marbles." Collectively, the reporters were called Murrow's Boys and are credited with inventing the broadcast-journalism style that has carried over to television news.

The world edged closer to war. A few months later, in September 1938, Hitler precipitated another crisis by threatening to annex the Sudetenland, an area of Czechoslovakia inhabited by many people of German heritage. For most of that month a nervous world held its collective breath as European leaders tried to avoid war. Prime Minister Neville Chamberlain of Great Britain flew to Munich to negotiate peace with Hitler. When he returned to England with the joyous announcement that he and Hitler had agreed on "peace in our time," the world breathed a sigh of relief. Others, more realistic, knew this was only a temporary interlude on the road to all-out war.

In the United States, too, people followed the story of the "Munich Crisis" with great interest. While NBC's Max Jordan in Berlin used his many contacts in the German government to report on the happenings, it was CBS's H. V. Kaltenborn in New York who helped Americans understand the complexity of the situation. For twenty days of the crisis Kaltenborn did not leave his New York studio. He slept, when he could, on a cot and made over one hundred separate broadcasts analyzing news reports from the freshly assembled CBS reporters in Europe and the wire-service stories that were fed into the studio. He analyzed everything he heard, once even including a prayer offered by the archbishop of Canterbury.

The *Anschluss* and Munich Crisis prepared the way for American radio to cover World War II. Before 1938 radio did nothing more than use wire-service and newspaper reports; now, with Murrow and his boys in the forefront, Americans began to rely on the new style of broadcast journalism to keep them informed of quickly changing political and military conditions. Around the country anxious people turned on their radios to hear "Calling Edward Murrow: Come in, Ed Murrow." Americans still read newspapers, but an article in *Scribners Magazine* in 1938 listed three advantages Murrow had over his newspaper colleagues:

1. He beat the newspapers by hours.
2. He reached millions who otherwise would have had to depend on local papers for their foreign news.
3. He wrote his own headlines; he emphasized what he wished.

Chamberlain's visit to Hitler only bought time, not peace. During this relatively quiet interlude, radio journalists brought the feelings of false security home to America. From Germany there was "Hello, NBC, Max Jordan calling from Bunkershausen." And from France, Eric Sevareid reported for CBS on the Maginot Line, the defensive fortification designed to keep Germany from attacking.

For the first time ever, Americans were able to experience a war firsthand, with a realism that only television would surpass, a decade later. When Edward R. Murrow first arrived in England for CBS in 1937, he told the head of the British Broadcasting Corporation, "I want our programs to be anything but intellectual. I want them to be down to earth, in the vernacular of the man in the street." When war finally came, that was the credo Murrow followed. He brought the horror and anguish of a European war home to American living rooms.

During the Battle of Britain in 1940, as German bombs fell upon London with devastating results, Murrow broadcast continuously to America. The United States had not yet entered the war and was technically neutral. Murrow's personal accounts of British endurance during the onslaught created great sympathy for England's plight and prepared American public opinion for involvement in the war against Germany.

As the bombs fell, Murrow took great personal risks as he broad-

Representatives of the major American networks at Supreme Allied Headquarters in London during World War II. Edward R. Murrow is second from right. *National Archives.*

cast to America. "Five times in ten blocks I've gone flat on the pavement . . . the individual's reaction to the sound of falling bombs cannot be described. That moan of stark terror and suspense cannot be encompassed by words." He stood on rooftops to better report on enemy bombing and only entered underground air-raid shelters to report on conditions there. When his colleague Larry LeSueur expressed concern about the risks, Murrow, LeSueur recalled, simply advised him that if he were out during a bombing he should just "lie flat in the gutter, head down, mouth open, and hands over ears."

When German bombs directly hit the headquarters of the British Broadcasting Corporation, from whose underground studios Murrow was broadcasting, he told his listeners, "I can tell you from personal experience that it's not pleasant to sit in a studio filled with the odor of iodine and antiseptics and talk to you, at home, while good friends are being carried on stretchers along the corridor outside the studio door."

In the early days of the war the networks remained leery of recorded programs—everything had to be live. The success of a broadcast depended very much on timing and ingenuity to put across an intended message. "One night, just as one of these programs was scheduled to begin, the sirens sounded for one of the first air raids. A microphone was held level with the pavement, and listeners all over America could hear the calm, unhurried footsteps of Londoners while the sirens howled in the background." The network later boasted: "That combination of sound did more than pages of print or hours of radio news reporting to convince America that Londoners took their air raids without excitement or panic."

Americans looked forward to Murrow's broadcasts. Each began with the simple words, "This is London." The manner in which he pronounced those three words, with an emphasis on the first word and a distinct delivery that commanded attention, became his trademark. His This-is-London broadcasts created mental images at home in

America of what life was like for the suffering British in the subways, air-raid shelters, pubs, and businesses. His reports, like those of his CBS colleagues, were never hysterical, in sound or content. He relied on the use of short sentences and a dignified, measured delivery to present his information. His speech classes at Washington State College had taught him well, as these excerpts from his wartime broadcasts show.

> This is London at half past three in the morning. The air raid over the London area is still in progress. . . . No words of mine can describe the spectacle over London tonight, so I'll talk about the people underground. . . .
>
> Just overhead now, the burst of the antiaircraft fire. . . . Now you'll hear two bursts a little nearer. . . . There they are! That hard, stony sound.
>
> Stumbling through the darkness, there is time to think of British courtesy as well as courage, the good-humored courtesy of taxi drivers and bus conductors, of people who still thank you for asking them to do you a favor, even when it's hard to hear their thanks above the roar of the guns.

He reported from a British minesweeper in the English Channel:

> It was rough and wet out there today . . . the wind had freshened and our little trawler was taking plenty of water aboard. . . . Heroes aren't expensive in Britain's most famous minesweeping patrol, but it takes plenty of four-o'clock-in-the-morning courage to do that job.

He spent a night with London's fire department:

> I must have seen well over a hundred firebombs come down. We picked a fire from the map and drove to it. . . . And back at headquarters I saw a man laboriously and carefully copying names in a big ledger—the list of firemen killed in action during the last month.

He stood alone with his microphone on London rooftops during air raids:

> This is London. I'm standing again tonight on a rooftop looking out over London, feeling rather large and lonesome. In the first of the last fifteen or twenty minutes, there's been considerable action up here. But at the moment there's an ominous silence hanging over London. But at the same time a silence that has a great deal of dignity. Just straightaway in front of me the search-

Edward R. Murrow in London broadcasting news of the Allied invasion of France. A British censor sits with his finger on a button that would cut off the program in midsentence if anything Murrow said might damage wartime security. The button was never used. *National Archives.*

lights are working. . . . Just on the roof across the way I can see a man standing, wearing a tin hat, a pair of powerful night glasses to his eyes, scanning the sky. Again, looking in the opposite direction, there's a building with two windows gone. Out of one window there waves something that looks like a white bed sheet, a window curtain swinging free in this night breeze. It looks as though it were being shaken by a ghost. There are a great many ghosts around these buildings in London. In some of them, companies of ghosts.

He joined common folks in the underground air-raid shelters:

There are no words to describe the thing that is happening. The courage of the people, the flash and roar of the guns rolling down the streets, the stench of the air-raid shelter. In three or four hours people must get up and go to work just as though they had a full night's rest, free from the rumble of guns and wonder that comes when they wake and listen in the dead hours of the night.

He went on a Royal Air Force bombing raid over Berlin, in which forty-one bombers were lost, to make his award-winning report on the "orchestrated hell" he witnessed:

This is London. Yesterday afternoon, the waiting was over; the weather was right; the target was to be the big city. "D for Dog" [the plane's designation] eased around the perimeter track to the end of the runway. We sat there for a moment. The green light flashed and we were rolling—ten seconds ahead of schedule! The takeoff was smooth as silk. The wheels came up and "D for Dog" started the long climb. As we came up through the clouds, I looked right and left, and counted fourteen black Lancasters climbing for the place where men must burn oxygen to live. The sun was going down and its red glow made rivers and lakes of fire on the tops of the clouds. Down to the southward, the clouds piled up to form castles, battlements, and whole cities—all tinged with red. . . .

The small incendiaries were going down like a fistful of white rice thrown on a piece of black velvet. As Jock hauled the "Dog" up again, I was thrown to the other side of the cockpit, and there below were more incendiaries, glowing white and then turning red. The cookies—the four-thousand-pound high explosives— were bursting below like great sunflowers gone mad. And then, as we started down again, still held in the lights, I remembered that the "Dog" still had one of those cookies and a whole basket of incendiaries in his belly and the lights still held us. And I was very frightened.

The bomb doors were open. Boz called his directions, "Five left, five left" and then there was a gentle, confident, upward thrust under my feet and Boz said, "Cookie gone." A few seconds later, the incendiaries went and "D-Dog" seemed lighter and easier to handle. I began to reflect again that all men would be brave if only they could leave their stomachs at home. . . .

Berlin was a kind of orchestrated hell, a terrible symphony of light and flame. It isn't a pleasant kind of warfare—the men doing it speak of it as a job. . . . Men die in the sky while others are roasted alive in their cellars. Berlin last night was not a pretty sight.

Murrow was one of the first reporters to enter a Nazi concentration camp—Buchenwald—at the war's conclusion. He was so horrified that he doubted he could properly report on what he saw.

When I entered, men crowded around, tried to lift me to their shoulders. They were too weak. . . . As we walked out into the courtyard a man fell dead. . . . In another part of the camp they showed me the children. Hundreds of them; some were only six. . . . There were two rows of bodies, stacked up like cord-wood . . . it appeared that most of the men and boys had died of starvation. . . . I have reported what I saw and heard, but only part of it. If I have offended you by this rather mild account of Buchenwald, I am not in the least sorry.

Years later, radio and television broadcast wars from Korea, Vietnam, and the Persian Gulf into homes around the world. But World War II was the first war in history broadcast to the world by radio. It did not make warfare less bloody, but no longer were there long time-gaps between an event and public awareness of it. It brought the reality of distant war directly into people's homes. Throughout the war years, and in spite of military censorship, the familiar voices of the radio correspondents assured people that they were hearing the truth. No home was without its radio and no radio was without listeners constantly tuned in for the latest news from the battlefront. Like no other medium before it, radio brought the country together by providing a shared experience of unfolding events.

Political and military leaders spoke directly to the people at home, as President Roosevelt did in his fireside chats and formal addresses to Congress. Radio reporters were attached to the military as official war correspondents with access to all kinds of news, with restrictions, of course, for military security. NBC presented a weekly "Army Hour" that featured on-the-scene reports from around the world. On D day, when Allied troops landed on the coast of France to begin the war's major offensive against Germany, radio was there to report the scenes to the American public. For the families at home, being connected to events around the world made it easier to accept the fact that sons, brothers, husbands, and fathers were fighting, some never to return.

Throughout the war, the news roundup invented by Murrow and CBS during the *Anschluss* daily provided listeners with direct reports from major fronts. Even after the war, CBS continued to successfully use this news format morning and night. During the war, efforts were made to cover the news from all fronts, but broadcasters seemed to do a better job covering the European war than the war with Japan. A lot of this had to do with the fact that for years Americans were more interested in Europe than the Orient, and consequently more news agencies were established in Europe. A simpler reason was the state of technology at the time. Since broadcasts were dependent upon shortwave transmissions, it was easier to communicate over the Atlantic than the wider Pacific.

There were approximately five hundred American journalists in England during the war; fewer than fifty of them were radio correspondents. In the words of the American ambassador to Great Britain John Gilbert Winant, "They accepted discomforts and risked life cheerfully in their determined effort to keep the American people informed."

In December 1940, on a visit home after covering the Battle of Britain, Edward R. Murrow was tendered a lavish dinner in the grand ballroom of New York's Waldorf-Astoria Hotel. After the meal, Archibald MacLeish, the librarian of congress, rose to address the group. Turning to the guest of honor, the noted scholar eloquently spoke of what Murrow's reports had done for the American people: "You destroyed a superstition . . . the superstition that what is done beyond three thousand miles of water is not really done at all. . . . You burned the city of London in our houses, and we felt the flames that burned it. You laid the dead of London at our doors."

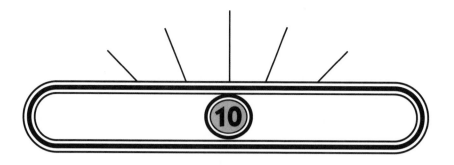

"Say Good Night, Gracie"

Now we add sight to sound.

DAVID SARNOFF, 1939

In 1945, at the end of World War II, more American homes had radios than bathtubs. Radio helped Americans survive and cope with the tumultuous upheavals of the 1930s and 1940s—from the despair of the Great Depression through the heartache of the Second World War. It was precisely because times were so perilous that people needed an escape from hunger, unemployment, and war. From 1930 through 1945, the golden age of radio and its legendary personalities offered that escape.

The welcome and familiar voices of America's great entertainers brought daily comfort and continuity into homes all across the country. At the time of World War II, most American homes had at least one radio. Battery-operated portable and automobile radios became popular, and listeners were never far away from their favorite programs. The unseen men and women of the airwaves soon became more than heroes: They were welcome household guests. Their unique comedy, music, and patter helped people temporarily forget their daily problems and made life more bearable.

With the development of radio news, the country had instant knowledge of events around the world. Newspapers suffered circulation losses that eventually resulted in the closing of thousands of newspapers. Live broadcasts of important events and access to instant information made Americans participants in history rather than observers. When President Roosevelt spoke to the nation about events of the day, people felt he was personally confiding in them and, in turn, they supported his programs. Radio made Americans a more self-confident and uniform people, in thought, culture, and appearance. It provided everyone with common experiences that, at least on the outside, swept away visible differences. People used the same advertised products, followed the latest fads, and talked about the same programs.

Today radio is not dead, just different. In the 1930s a single radio, placed in the living room like a fine piece of furniture, was the center of family life. Today there are clock radios on our night tables, battery-operated sets on our belts as we jog, and radios in our automobiles. We enjoy the music, listen to the news, and argue with talk show hosts. We still depend on radio for news, but it provides only part of our overall electronic entertainment. The earlier power of radio to change our lives is gone, replaced in the early 1950s by a more advanced form of broadcasting—television.

The shift from sound to pictures was not as traumatic as one would have expected. The idea of broadcasting images existed even before the days of radio. Alexander Graham Bell, inventor of the telephone, was issued a patent for a television device back in 1880. Across the ocean, in England and in Russia, experimenters fiddled with tubes and machines to create a radio that broadcast sound and pictures. When Vladimir Zworykin emigrated to the United States from Russia in 1919, he quickly became RCA's most prominent television experimenter and is credited with creating the high-definition technology that made it all possible.

David Sarnoff, NBC's legendary head, constantly promoted RCA's efforts to create a workable television system. In 1923, in a memorandum reminiscent of his Radio Music Box letter anticipating the role of radio, Sarnoff predicted television. "I believe that television, which is the technical name for seeing instead of hearing by radio, will come to pass in due course." Again, Sarnoff proved to be prophetic.

Television experimentation was also going on at rival CBS. In 1932 that network actually broadcast forty hours of television programming a week. Unfortunately, except for the few experimental television sets with tiny square screens, few could receive the grainy broadcasts of Ed Sullivan or Arthur Godfrey. Things were a little better in England. A visitor to Edward R. Murrow's London apartment in 1937 later recounted in amazement having watched a movie broadcast by the BBC on a small-screen set.

Television was the greatest hit of New York's 1939 World's Fair. Sarnoff himself opened the exhibit, the first large-scale public demonstration of this new broadcasting medium. His simple statement "Now we add sight to sound" did not do justice to the powerful impact television would make on the world.

But first, there was World War II. The war pushed further thoughts about television temporarily into the background. But once the war ended, the major American networks picked up where they had left off. In 1946 there were fewer than twenty thousand television sets in the country; by the end of 1949 factories were mass-producing over a quarter of a million sets a month. Two years later, sales of televisions overtook radios. There was no turning back. By the early 1950s even soap operas began the move from radio to television.

From the first, the networks plunged into programming in a big way. In 1948 there were forty television stations covering twenty-five American cities from coast to coast. That year's presidential conventions were covered live. Just as the first convention broadcast by radio in the 1920s changed public awareness of politics, television made the process even more realistic. Viewers at home could not only hear what was going on, but also were able to look at the organized pandemonium for themselves.

Just as early radio broadcasts patterned themselves after existing entertainment forms, television drew upon lessons learned from nearly thirty years of radio. One pioneer television executive complained that the medium was not being used to its fullest potential, since the major stars seemed to be simply imitating radio. Just as the earliest radio personalities drew from their vaudeville roots, the early television stars came from radio.

Stars whose vaudeville training had taught them to rely on sight gags, outlandish costumes, and exaggerated motions easily transferred their talents to television. Milton Berle, never a great radio personality, became an overnight television sensation. His vaudeville slapstick and visual humor made "Uncle Miltie" a viewing must: He was "Mr. Television." Just as people had changed their schedules to be home in time for "Amos 'n' Andy" two decades earlier, families gathered in front of the television every Tuesday evening at eight for Berle's "Texaco Star Theater." In some ways television changed the way Americans lived. The television—families usually had just one—was centrally located so that family members could sit comfortably and watch. Guests who did not own sets yet were invited (or invited themselves) to watch this technological wonder. As movie theaters lost customers and radio listening declined, television became the center of American life.

Arthur Godfrey, so successful on radio because of his easygoing manner and quick wit, simply transferred his style to television. The only difference was that now his fans could see him talk. Ed Wynn, who had insisted on dressing up in clownish costumes and hats to broadcast to an unseen radio audience, gloried in television. A review of his first radio broadcast in 1932, by an anonymous listener, incorrectly underestimated Wynn's need to perform in front of an audience: "This ever funny clown, of course, does not come into the category of those who have to be seen in order to be fully appreciated." The listener at home never knew what was going on in the studio!

Other radio stars easily made the transfer from radio to television. Ed Sullivan, a newspaper columnist who began his radio career as an interviewer, hosted the long-running television variety show "Toast of the Town." Jack Benny's program ran for sixteen years with the same cast of characters who had made his radio show such a success. George Burns and Gracie Allen also had a successfully long run on television. The story lines revolved around situations that were acted out much like plays, with the same fresh and witty styles that had worked so well on radio. The only difference was that families seated in living rooms could now watch their favorite entertainers perform. When George Burns turned to his wife at the end of each program with his "Say good night, Gracie," viewers could see the famous exchange for themselves.

"Amos 'n' Andy" underwent change of a different kind when it reached television. Gosden and Correll, the two white men who invented the African-American radio characters in the 1920s, gave way to an all African-American cast for television. By the early 1950s, the program was still popular, in spite of the growing number of objections to its stereotyped portrayals. It did, however, provide African-American actors with much-needed exposure on television. There were few black Americans in radio and fewer still on television.

As people listened to radio, they used their imaginations to picture the stars and their actions. Everyone knew that sound effects and scripts were used, yet somehow these broadcasts seemed real. In 1937 nearly one and a half million people attended live radio broadcasts to see the magic as it was created. Like the listeners at home, they relied on their imaginations to visualize the scenes. Television shattered the illusions.

The family radio was more than a piece of furniture, it was a magical link to an enchanted world of entertainment, news, and culture. By the mid-1930s the radio was the most important item in the home. It provided shared experiences to everyone, rich and poor, city dweller and farmer, black and white, educated and illiterate. The programs and the advertising created an image of an ideal America beyond the problems of poverty, war, and race. It made radio performers national heroes.

There was something to satisfy every interest. For fans of country and western music, there was "The Grand Ole Opry." For opera fans, the Metropolitan Opera, presented by Texaco, was a Saturday-afternoon tradition. The "Lux Radio Theater" presented Hollywood's leading actors and actresses in plays by well-known writers. CBS's "School of the Air" was an educational mainstay of the network for years. William Paley, the longtime president of CBS, pointed out that at one time 75 percent of his network's programming in the 1930s was devoted to cultural subjects. NBC, not to be outdone, hired world-famous conductor Arturo Toscanini to conduct the NBC Symphony Orchestra. Baseball, football, and boxing were welcomed into homes across the country as the voices of sportscasters like Red Barber became familiar to millions of listeners.

Radio proved its ultimate worth during World War II when it demonstrated the value of news. Before the war, news programming accounted for less than 5 percent of daily broadcasts. During the conflict, that figure jumped to over 30 percent as people depended on radio news to keep them informed and connected to world events. The commentators became national celebrities; their voices and names were among the most recognized in the nation. Only President Roosevelt was better known, and he became a radio personality in his own right.

On October 30, 1938, people listening to their radios grew hysterical with fright. The impossible had happened and radio was announcing it live—the Martians had landed and were destroying

NBC staged a coup when it engaged the famous conductor Arturo Toscanini to lead its own NBC Symphony Orchestra. *American Library of Radio and Television, Thousand Oaks Library.*

everything in sight. "News reports" from a small New Jersey town confirmed the initial scare, and people fled their homes to save their lives. It took a while to convince everyone that what they had been listening to was a radio adaptation of the science fiction classic *War of the Worlds* on CBS's "Mercury Theater of the Air" hosted by Orson Welles. Some lay blame for the evening's mass hysteria on nerves strained to the breaking point by radio reports of Nazi activity in Europe. Orson Welles had unknowingly tapped a raw nerve.

Echoes of the old radio programs can be heard today. There has been a growing interest in recent years in the old shows that shaped modern broadcasting. Cassettes of long-forgotten programs and personalities are readily available in libraries and bookstores and are heard on an increasing number of radio stations. They are bringing laughs and thrills to a new generation of listeners.

Yet, while we today can still enjoy the humor of Jack Benny, the thrills of "The Green Hornet," and the soapy tears of "Our Gal Sunday," we can only begin to imagine what the early days of radio meant for people who actually experienced them.

Select Bibliography

Barnouw, Erik. *A History of Broadcasting in the United States,* 3 vols. New York: Oxford University Press, 1968.

———. *The Sponsor.* New York: Oxford University Press, 1978.

Benny, Joan. *Sunday Nights at Seven.* New York: Warner, 1990.

Bliss, Edward J. *Now the News.* New York: Columbia University Press, 1991.

Buxton, Frank, and Bill Owen. *The Big Broadcast.* New York: Viking Press, 1963.

Campbell, Robert. *The Golden Years of Broadcasting.* New York: Charles Scribner's Sons, 1976.

Culbert, David. *News for Everyman.* Westport, Conn.: Greenwood Press, 1976.

Douglas, George. *The Early Days of Broadcasting.* Jefferson, N.C.: McFarland, 1987.

Dunning, John. *Tune in Yesterday.* Englewood Cliffs, N.J.: Prentice-Hall, 1976.

Edmondson, Madeleine, and David Rounds. *From Mary Noble to Mary Hartman.* New York: Stein and Day, 1976.

Harmon, Jim. *The Great Radio Comedians.* Garden City, N.Y.: Doubleday, 1970.

———. *The Great Radio Heroes.* Garden City, N.Y.: Doubleday, 1967.

Henderson, Amy. *On the Air.* Washington: Smithsonian Institution Press, 1988.

Kendrick, Alexander. *Prime Time.* Boston: Little Brown, 1969.

Lackman, Ron. *Remember Radio.* New York: G. P. Putnam's Sons, 1970.

Lyons, Eugene. *David Sarnoff.* New York: Harper & Row, 1966.

MacDonald, J. Fred. *Don't Touch That Dial.* Chicago: Nelson-Hall, 1979.

Persico, Joseph. *Edward R. Murrow.* New York: McGraw-Hill, 1988.

Settel, Irving. *A Pictorial History of Radio.* New York: Grosset and Dunlap, 1967.

Smith, Sally. *In All His Glory: The Life of William S. Paley.* New York: Simon and Schuster, 1990.

Sperber, A. M. *Murrow.* New York: Freundlich, 1986.

Thomas, Lowell. *Good Evening Everybody.* New York: William Morrow, 1976.

Index

Index